Aging and the Aged

Also of Interest

Violence and the Family, edited by Maurice R. Green

Life Course: Integrative Theories and Exemplary Populations, edited by Kurt W. Back

Aging from Birth to Death: Interdisciplinary Perspectives, edited by Matilda White Riley

A Practical Guide to the Conduct of Field Research in the Social Sciences, Elliot J. Feldman

The Dynamics of Aging: Original Essays on the Processes and Experiences of Growing Old, Forrest J. Berghorn, Donna E. Schafer, and Associates

Prisoners of Space? Exploring the Geographical Experience of Older People, Graham D. Rowles

Health for the Whole Person: The Complete Guide to Holistic Medicine, Arthur C. Hastings, James Fadiman, and James S. Gordon

New Space for Women, edited by Gerda R. Wekerle, Rebecca Peterson, and David Morley

Westview Guides to Library Research
Robert K. Baker, Series Editor

Aging and the Aged:
An Annotated Bibliography and
Library Research Guide
Linna Funk Place
Linda Parker
Forrest J. Berghorn

Designed to introduce undergraduates to library research in the field of gerontology, this book stresses both general reference works and those materials that present state-of-the-art discussions of important issues. The interdisciplinary nature of the study of aging is emphasized throughout the bibliography, and attention is given to the wide variety of sources available for research. In general, the book's subject areas are designed to correspond to those in THE DYNAMICS OF AGING (Berghorn, Schafer, and Associates, Westview Press, 1981).

Linna Funk Place, a member of the Humanities Advisory Board of the National Council on Aging, teaches history at the University of Missouri-Kansas City and is a Ph.D. candidate in American studies at the University of Kansas. Linda Parker is reference librarian for women's studies, University Libraries, University of Wisconsin. Forrest J. Berghorn is associate professor of American studies and assistant director of the Gerontology Center, University of Kansas.

Aging and the Aged:
An Annotated Bibliography and Library Research Guide

Linna Funk Place
Linda Parker
Forrest J. Berghorn

Westview Press / Boulder, Colorado

Westview Guides to Library Research

Copyright © 1981 by Westview Press, Inc.

Published in 1981 in the United States of America by
    Westview Press, Inc.
    5500 Central Avenue
    Boulder, Colorado 80301
    Frederick A. Praeger, Publisher

Library of Congress Cataloging in Publication Data
Place, Linna Funk.
    Aging and the aged.
    (Westview guides to library research)
    Includes indexes.
    1. Gerontology--Bibliography. I. Parker, Linda, joint author. II. Berghorn,
Forrest J., 1932-   joint author. III. Title.
Z7164.04P52 (HQ10)   016.3052'6   80-20763
ISBN 0-89158-934-1

Composition for this book was provided by the authors.
Printed and bound in the United States of America.

Contents

Preface

Interest in gerontology--i.e., the study of old age and aging processes--is growing rapidly. An increasing number of students are either preparing for or contemplating careers in gerontology, careers that may proceed through the scholarly disciplines, the service professions, or positions in government. Whatever the career choice, students of gerontology will need to develop individual skills that will enable them to acquire an adequate knowledge of this complex field of study. Such skills will also prove valuable to those who are not formally students but who are interested in acquiring a greater understanding of old age and aging for personal reasons. The principal purpose of this book is to introduce readers to the basic literature in the field and to help them use the tools of library research effectively.

Gerontology is a relatively young area of investigation that draws on the investigative procedures and accumulated knowledge of many disciplines. For just a few examples: part of our understanding of the consequences of growing old is based on the experimental evidence of biologists and psychologists; much of what we know about attitudes toward old age derives from the surveys of sociologists; and our knowledge of the ethnic factor in aging owes a great deal to the cross-cultural analyses of anthropologists. The comparatively recent development of gerontology and its multidisciplinary nature have, to some extent, influenced the content of this volume.

It has become something of a convention to include only books and full-length monographs in bibliographies such as this. However, we have chosen to include also a number of anthologies and journal articles that are particularly useful

introductions to the field. To exclude such works,
one runs the risk of omitting the most representative writing of some prominent gerontologists.
Moreover, among the sub-fields of gerontology are
those--ethnicity and aging, for instance--that have
only recently emerged, and their major concepts and
findings are at the present time most clearly
articulated in journal articles or in collections
of articles.

While the authors have taken into account the
multidisciplinary nature of gerontological scholar-
ship, we have not structured the bibliography
exclusively along disciplinary lines. Rather, we
have organized the scholarly literature according
to several salient, and broadly defined, subject
areas: physiological and psychological aspects of
aging; social aspects of aging; and environmental
aspects of aging.

In general, we have attempted to compile a
"teaching" bibliography, one that will be as helpful to those who are just beginning their studies as
it is to more advanced students. As such, it is not
meant to be definitive. Rather, it is a selected
bibliography, and the selections collectively are
intended to answer the question: What writings in
gerontology constitute a solid introduction to the
field or to a sub-field of particular interest?

L. F. P.
L. P.
F. J. B.
Lawrence, Kansas

Acknowledgments

In developing a bibliography that cuts across disciplinary lines, it is necessary to enlist the aid of many people who possess knowledge of specific areas of study. We would like to express our appreciation to the following people who cheerfully responded to our request for assistance: Janet Barber, David Berland, David Campbell, Allan Cigler, Dennis Dailey, K. Anthony Edwards, Jacob Gordon, David Hardcastle, Charles Longino, Jr., Mary Jane Moore, Wayne Osness, Shirley Patterson, and Geoffrey Steere. We also would like to thank Sue Schumock for her assistance in preparing the final copy of the manuscript.

1
The Library in
Gerontological Research

The purpose of this chapter is to help develop
skills which will enable one to find information
about aging, the aged, and the field of gerontology
in a college or university library. By developing
a strategy for locating materials, students will
spend time and energy in the most efficient manner.

How do you develop this strategy? The major
tools that a researcher uses include the card
catalog and guides to the literature (e.g., subject
bibliographies and periodical indexes). The card
catalog is arranged in alphabetical order by author,
title, and subject. Some libraries will file author,
title, and subject cards in one alphabetical
sequence in the same catalog; other libraries will
file authors and titles in one catalog, and subjects
in a separate arrangement. Ask the reference
librarian which system is used in your library.

The cards for each book contain a wealth of
information which will help you determine whether or
not a particular item fits your research needs. The
important data to look for are the bibliographic
description, subject headings, and the classification (or call) number. The following illustration
identifies the parts of a library catalog card,* and
contains hints for evaluating a book.

---

*Numbers (bold face) have been added to more
clearly identify the various parts.

9 HQ 1 Atchley, Robert C.
1061   2 The social forces in later life. 3 Belmont, CA:
A78   Wadsworth, 1977.
1977   4 413 pp. 23 cm. 5 (Lifetime series in aging)
       6 Bibliography. Includes Index

       7 1. Gerontology. 2. Aged-United States. 3. Retire-
       ment. United States. 8 I. Title.

1. AUTHOR ENTRY. What is the reputation of the
author? Has she/he written books on similar topics?

2. TITLE AND SUBTITLE. Is the title descriptive--
that is, does it give an indication of the contents?

3. IMPRINT (place of publication, publisher, date
of publication). Is the publisher reliable? (One
may consult professors and librarians about the
reputation of individual publishers concerning the
quality and reliability of data.) What is the date
of the book? Do you need recent information only?
Can you use an older book for historical perspective?

4. COLLATION (the physical description of the
book). This line indicates the number of pages,
illustrations, and the actual size in centimeters.
The length of the book may indicate its
comprehensiveness.

5. SERIES (a collection of books on a similar
topic produced by the same publisher). The title
which appears in parentheses after the collation
indicates the series to which the book belongs.
Could other books in the same series be relevant
to your topic? What is the reputation of the
authors of other books in the same series?

6. BIBLIOGRAPHIC NOTES. The notes indicate whether
a book has bibliographies either at the end of each
chapter or at the end of the book. These
bibliographies provide invaluable clues to other
sources of information.

7. & 8. TRACINGS (other entries under which
catalog cards are filed for this particular book).
The entries following the Arabic number are the
subject headings assigned to the book, while the
entries following the Roman numerals list the
additional authors and title cards filed in the
catalog. Are these subjects relevant to your topic?
Do you see new subjects which you had not considered
before?

9. CLASSIFICATION NUMBER. The classification
(or call) number is assigned according to the
subject of the book and indicates the area in the
library where the book can be found.
     For their card catalogs, many libraries use
subject headings developed by the Library of
Congress. If you consult the book in which these
headings are listed alphabetically, Library of
Congress Subject Headings, you will be able to
develop a master list of subject headings which you
can use in the card catalog, periodical indexes, and
many book length bibliographies. The following
example is from the 1974-1976 cumulated supplement
to the Library of Congress Subject Headings and
shows how you can develop a list of headings.

> **Gerontology** *(HQ1060)*
>   *sa* Aged
>   Aging
>   Geriatrics
>   Old age
>   *xx* Geriatrics
>   Social sciences
>   — Addresses, essays, lectures
>   *x* Aged—Addresses, essays, lectures
>   — Collected works
>   *x* Aged—Collected works
>   — Congresses
>   *x* Aged—Congresses
>   — Periodicals
>   Here are entered periodicals on the
>   subject of the aged and their prob-
>   lems. Periodicals issued for the aged
>   on the problems of the aged are en-
>   tered under Aged—Periodicals.
>   *Note under* Aged—Periodicals
>   — Yearbooks
>   *x* Aged—Yearbooks

     Begin with the term GERONTOLOGY. It appears in
heavy black print which is an indication that this
is the primary term. Immediately under GERONTOLOGY
is the code sa followed by AGED, AGING, GERIATRICS,
and OLD AGE. The code sa means see also; therefore,
the words following sa are terms related to
GERONTOLOGY which could prove useful in helping you

to find additional information under slightly different categories of the main entry. GERONTOLOGY itself is subdivided and the subdivisions follow dashes. For example, "GERONTOLOGY--Periodicals" is the subject heading that you would consult in the card catalog in order to find out which periodicals on the subject of aging are owned by your library.

   The titles of magazines and periodicals are usually listed in the card catalog of a university or college library. However, the authors and titles of individual articles in the periodicals are not filed in the catalog, which is primarily a listing of the books in the library. In order to find out who has written articles in gerontology, you should consult indexes to periodical literature. Some indexes will give you the basic bibliographic citation (author, title, name of journal, volume, date, and page numbers) arranged under subject headings. For example, see the sample entry from the Social Sciences Index.

Aged
   See also
Aging
Attitudes toward the aged
Children and the aged
Indians of North America—Aged
Municipal services for the aged
Old age
Retirement
Retirement income
Social work with the aged
   Adjustment
Activity group experience for disengaged elderly persons. J. E. Harris and J. L. Bodden. bibl J Counsel Psychol 25:325-30 Jl '78
Autonomy: a continuing developmental task. S. E. Dresen. Am J Nursing 78:1344-6 Ag '78
Differential effects of relocation on nursing home patients. C. J. Pino and others. Gerontologist 18:167-72 Ap '78
Dignity in aging: notes on geriatric ethics [with reply by E. L. Menkin] D. Christiansen. bibl J Humanistic Psychol 18:41-56 Spr '78
Empirical typology of adjustment to aging. E. Filsinger and W. J. Sauer. bibl J Gerontol 33:437-45 My '78
Factors contributing to older persons' satisfaction with their communities. R. Toseland and J. Rasch. bibl Gerontologist 18:395-402 Ag '78

Gerontologists, Professional ethics for
Ethical issues related to research involving elderly subjects. W. T. Reich. bibl Gerontologist 18:326-37 Ag '78
Gerontology
Impending society of immortals [with scenarios of the future]. J. Fowles. il Futurist 12:175-81 Je '78
Planning for the elderly [symposium]. ed. by M. E. Wolfgang. Am Acad Pol & Soc Sci Ann 438:1-107 Jl '78
Symposium: role of humanities in gerontology. ed. by D. D. Van Tassel. Gerontologist 18:574-83 D '78
   See also
Aged
   Abstracts
Abstracts of papers and posters to be presented at the 31st scientific meeting of the Gerontological society. Gerontologist 18:43-174 O pt2 '78

Bibliography
Current publications in gerontology and geriatrics. comp. by
N. W. Shock. See issues of Journal of gerontology
Methodology
Statistical methods
Principles for identifying structural differences; some me-
thodological issues related to comparative factor analysis.
W. R. Cunningham. bibl J Gerontol 33:82-6 Ja '78
Survey research in aging: an evaluation of the Harris survey.
J. C. Henretta and others. bibl Gerontologist 17:160-7 Ap
'77; Discussion. 18:64-6, 588-90 F, D '78
Philosophy
Essay: gerontology's search for understanding. R. Kasten-
baum. Gerontologist 18:59-63 F '78
Open letter [with reply by G. L. Maddox]. M. Kuhn. il Geron-
tologist 18:422-7 O pt 1 '78

Other indexes will provide an annotation or abstract
(a brief description of the article). The following
example is an entry from the Current Index to
Journals in Education. The typical format for an
index which uses abstracts usually includes a
separate subject section which gives you a
reference number to look up in a main entry section.
The subject term is AGING and has references to two
articles. The entry number for the first article,
"Group Counseling for the Elderly," is EJ 209 155.

Aging
Group Counseling for the Elderly. *Journal for Specialists in
Group Work;* v4 n3 p148-54 Sum 1979   EJ 209 155
Attitude Change in Older Age: An Experimental Study.
Journal of Gerontology; v34 n5 p697-703 Sep 1979
EJ 209 175

When you look up this number in the main entry
section, you find, in addition to the bibliographic
citation, a list of the subject headings assigned to
the article and a brief annotation summarizing the
content of the article.

EJ 209 155   CG 516 757
Group Counseling for the Elderly. Capuzzi, Dave;
Fillion, Nancy G. *Journal for Specialists in Group
Work;* v4 n3 p148-54 Sum 1979 (Reprint: UMI)
Descriptors: *Age; Geriatrics; *Group Activities;
*Group Counseling; *Human Development;
Humanistic Education; Older Adults
Identifiers: *Aging
Purposes of the group counseling experience are to accept
the aging process as a natural consequence of living, to
promote understanding that a positive attitude toward ag-
ing can increase chances of enjoying later years, to provide
members with information about community resources,
and to develop a support system. (Author)

After you have chosen the articles which you
want to read, you must determine if your library
owns the journal which contains the article. In
addition to the title cards in the catalog, many
libraries have a list of the journals which they own.
This list will give you the call number, location,
and exact volume numbers and dates of the issues
held by the library. The following entry is from
the 1979 Union Catalog of Serials from the University

6

of Wisconsin-Madison. It informs the student that

Gerontologist. *(Washington, etc.)* ISSN
0016-9013
Social Work Library AP .G378 2
v. 1-to date; March 1961-to date.

the journal, <u>Gerontologist</u>, is located in the Social
Work Library, shelved under the classification
number, AP .G378 2, and that the Library owns a
complete set from volume 1, number 1 to the present
time. Using a library's journal list will save you
time and many false starts. Ask the librarian to
assist you in interpreting the list if you have any
questions.

Indexes to articles in journals and use of the
card catalog are two important methods for finding
information to use in research papers. A third step
in the search for data is to use bibliographies
which appear either as separately published books,
such as B. McIlvaine's <u>Aging: A Guide to Reference
Sources, Journals and Government Publications</u>, or
as articles in journals, such as M. Delgado's
"Spanish-speaking Elderly; A Bibliography,"
<u>Gerontologist</u>, 18 (August 1978), 387-394. The
reference librarian will assist you in finding
these sources in the reference collection. The
following bibliography will also aid you. It is
a list of reference books which should be available
in most libraries and which will provide you with
citations to books, articles, films, and other types
of library materials about aging. The first
category, REFERENCE BOOKS, includes a list of
interdisciplinary materials which have a high degree
of relevance for the field of gerontology. The
next category includes bibliographies on a number of
the topics associated with the study of aging. This
is followed by three additional listings: handbooks
and directories; selected journals; and private and
public organizations and associations in gerontology.

REFERENCE BOOKS

American Reference Books Annual. Littleton, CO:
    Libraries Unlimited, 1970- .
    An annotated bibliography of new reference
books published during a year. It provides a
description of the strengths and weaknesses as well
as the main features of the book under review. It
is an excellent source for keeping up-to-date on new
reference books in gerontology.

Bibliographic Index. New York: H. W. Wilson, 1938-
    A subject index to bibliographies appearing
in parts of books, pamphlets, periodicals, or
published separately as books. Subjects covered
range from housing, medical care, and the
psychological aspects of aging to mass media and
the aged, transportation, and retirement income.

Books in Print. New York: Bowker, 1948- .
    A listing of books currently available for
sale from trade publishers in the United States.
It gives the source and price for buying the book.
There are separate volumes for authors, titles, and
subjects. Some representative subject headings for
gerontology are: 'Aged,' 'Aging,' 'Education of
the Aged,' 'Old Age,' 'Old Age Assistance,'
'Retirement,' 'Retirement Income.'

Current Index to Journals in Education. New York:
    CCM Information Sciences, 1969- .
    The Index covers more than 700 publications
in the field of education. It is the best source
for articles in education and related social
science fields. One can look up articles by author
or subject. Relevant subject headings include
'Older Adults,' 'Gerontology,' 'Adult Learning,'
'Senior Citizens,' 'Educational Gerontology,'
'Geriatrics,' 'Grandparents,' 'Personal Care Homes,'
'Retirement.'

Current Literature on the Aging. New York:
    National Council on the Aging, 1963- .
    A quarterly subject guide to selected publi-
cations in the field of aging and related areas.
It provides brief but informative annotations. The
majority of the citations are to professional and
scholarly sources. Some representative subject
terms include: 'Adult Education,' 'Bibliotherapy,'
'Ethnicity,' 'Life Cycle,' 'Pets,' 'Reality

Orientation,' 'Rural Population,' 'Self Help,'
'Women.' Annual, cumulative author and subject
indexes.

Editorial Research Reports. Washington, D.C.:
        Congressional Quarterly Inc., 1923- .
        Each report is organized into three sections--
(1) discussion of the importance of the subject
and major issues; (2) an in-depth examination of
background and historical developments; (3) a
discussion of future developments. The following
are reports on aging:

          Medical Aid to the Aged (4-20-60)
             Retirement Age (2-24-61)
       Nursing Homes and Medical Care (11-6-63)
                 Housing (7-22-64)
           Preparation for Medicare (12-8-65)
           Prolongation of Life (7-13-66)
        Social Security Improvements (12-14-66)
          Medical Costs and Medicare (5-24-67)
           Pension Plan Safeguards (9-20-67)
              Plight of the Aged (11-10-71)
          Social Security Financing (9-20-72)
            Retirement Security (12-27-74)
           Medicare and Medicaid (7-18-75)
              Pension Problems (5-21-76)
            Mandatory Retirement (11-11-77)

Encyclopedia of Associations. Detroit: Gale
        Research, 1980. 14th ed.
        Provides detailed information on nonprofit
American membership organizations of national scope.
Each entry includes name, address, size, objectives,
acronym of the organization, chief official and
title, founding date, purpose and activities of
organization, committees, sections and divisions,
publications, affiliated organizations, mergers
and changes of name, convention/meeting dates.
The Index is arranged by complete names of organizations and key words--e.g., 'Aged,' 'Aging,'
'Elderly,' 'Older Adult,' 'Older Women,' 'Retired,'
'Senior Citizens.'

Essay and General Literature Index. New York: H.
    W. Wilson, 1934- .
    An author and subject index to collections of
essays in the humanities and social sciences. It
includes subject headings such as 'Aged-psychology,'
'Old Age Research,' and 'Old Age Assistance.'

Ethel Percy Andrus Gerontology Center Library.
    Catalogs. Boston: G. K. Hall, 1976.
    Reproduction of the Center's card catalog.
The collection's emphasis is on social gerontology.
Types of material included in the catalog are books,
reports, conference proceedings, state and federal
documents, agency publications, and dissertations.
Vol. 1 is an author/title listing, v. 2, subjects.
Relevant subject areas are: psychology, sociology,
social welfare, biology, physiology, architecture,
environmental planning, geriatric nursing, housing,
and health care.

Gerontological Abstracts. Ann Arbor, MI: Univer-
    sity Information Services, 1972- .
    Indexes sources concerning the biological,
clinical, and social aspects of aging.

Human Resources Abstracts. Beverly Hills, CA:
    Sage Publications, 1966- .
    An index to human, social, and manpower problems
and solutions, poverty, and human resources
development. Relevant subject headings include
'Aged' and 'Social Security.'

Index Medicus. Washington, D.C.: National Library
    of Medicine, 1960- .
    A monthly subject bibliography of the
literature of biomedicine. It has references to
the social, political, and economic as well as
technical aspects of medicine. Some selected
subject headings are: 'Aged,' 'Health Insurance
for Aged and Disabled, Title 18,' 'Health Services
for the Aged,' 'Homes for the Aged,' 'Longevity,'
'Pensions,' 'Retirement,' 'Geriatrics,' 'Public
Assistance.'

Index to Articles by and about Blacks. Boston:
    G. K. Hall, 1950- .
    Author and subject index to Black American
periodicals. Consult the subject headings 'aged'
and 'retirement.'

International Federation on Aging. International
    Survey of Periodicals in Gerontology.
    Washington, D.C.: The Federation, 1978.
    A list of publications which are devoted
entirely to the subject of gerontology or which
regularly carry articles on aging. The entries
are arranged alphabetically by country. Each entry
is coded to indicate the appropriate audience--the
older person, providers of social services to the
elderly, health care professionals, or emphasis on
the biomedical aspects of aging. There is a title
index.

Monthly Catalog of United States Government
        Publications. Washington, D.C.: Government
        Printing Office, 1895- .
    The major index to federal publications from
all branches of government. It includes author,
title, subject, and series/report indexes. Some
relevant subject headings are: 'Aged,' 'Retirement,'
'Gerontology.'

Nutrition Abstracts and Reviews. Series A: Human
        and Experimental. Aberdeen, Scotland: Imperial
        Bureau of Animal Nutrition, 1931- .
    Published in the United Kingdom, this
bibliography lists many technical sources. It
contains a section titled, "Human Health and
Nutrition--Old Age."

Public Affairs Information Service Bulletin. New
        York: PAIS, 1915- .
    A broad, interdisciplinary index to periodical
articles, books, pamphlets, government documents,
covering contemporary social, economic, and political issues. There are useful entries found under:
'Old Age,' 'Senior Center,' 'Retirement,' and
'Pensions.'

Psychological Abstracts. Washington, D.C.:
        American Psychological Association, 1927- .
    Nonevaluative summaries (30-50 words long) of
the world's literature in psychology and related
disciplines. Some selected subject headings include:
'Aged (attitudes toward),' 'Physiological Aging,'
'Geriatric Patients,' 'Gerontology,' 'Middle Aged.'

Readers' Guide to Periodical Literature. New York:
        H. W. Wilson, 1905- .
    The widely used author and subject index to
periodicals of general interest. Subject headings

include: 'Gray Panthers (Pressure Group),'
'Physical Education for the Aged,' 'Aging,'
'Gerontology.'

Resources in Education. Washington, D.C.: U.S.
      Dept. of Health, Education, and Welfare, 1966-
      .
      A monthly abstracting service that announces
recent report literature related to the field of
education. It is an important tool for information
about the older adult. Subjects include:
'Gerontology,' 'Older Adults,' 'Educational
Gerontology,' 'Senior Citizens.'

Sheehy, Eugene P. Guide to Reference Books.
      Chicago: American Library Association, 1976.
      An annotated list of reference books basic to
research. It includes author, title, and subject
indexes. A good place to begin a literature search
is its section on 'Aging.'

Shock, Nathan W. A Classified Bibliography of
      Gerontology and Geriatrics. Stanford, CA:
      Stanford University Press, 1951. (Supplements
      1, 1949-1955; 2, 1956-1961)
      A total of 51,000 references to books and
journal articles from international sources. The
main categories are gerontology, general orientation, biology of aging, organ systems, geriatrics,
psychological processes, social and economic
aspects, and miscellaneous. There are author and
subject indexes.

Shock, Nathan W. "Current Publications in
      Gerontology and Geriatrics." Journal of
      Gerontology. 1950- .
      A regular feature in each bimonthly issue of the
Journal. It is one of the most important listings
of new books, journal articles, and government
documents in the fields of gerontology and
geriatrics. The arrangement is the same as in the
author's original bibliography (see above). There
is an annual author index, but no subject index.

Social Sciences Citation Index. Philadelphia:
      Institute for Scientific Information, 1969- .
      An international, multidisciplinary index to
the literature of the social, behavioral, and
related sciences. It has a search capability
through subject terms, author cited in a
bibliography of a current article, or author of a

current article. It is very useful in fields where
terminology is not standardized because subject
terms are the key words in the title of the article.
Since subject terms are not standardized, all forms
relating to a concept must be used--e.g., aged,
aging, elderly, geriatric.

Social Sciences Index. New York: H. W. Wilson,
     1907- . (Former titles: (1) International
     Index to Periodicals, (2) Social Sciences and
     Humanities Index).
     Author and subject index to English language
periodicals in anthropology, area studies,
economics, environmental sciences, geography, law
and criminology, medical sciences, political
science, psychology, public administration,
sociology. It also contains a section of citations
to book reviews. Representative subject headings
include: 'Attitudes toward the Aged,' 'Negro Aged,'
'Community Health Services for the Aged,' 'Nursing
Homes,' 'Alcohol and the Aged,' 'Aged as Consumers,'
'Aged in Television.'

Social Work Research and Abstracts. New York:
     National Association of Social Workers, 1965-
     Original research papers and abstracts of
articles in the field of social work technology,
research strategies, and analytical reviews of
research. Each issue has a major category on 'Aging
and the Aged.'

Sociological Abstracts. San Diego: Sociological
     Abstracts, Inc., 1952- .
     An index to the world's periodical articles in
sociology. Each entry is accompanied by an abstract.
There is an entire section devoted to social
gerontology. Selected subject headings include:
'Age,-ism,' 'Aging-Aged,' 'Gerontology,' 'Social
Security.' Beginning in 1978, each issue has a
detailed subject index. Previous years had a broad
subject index in each issue with the detailed
cumulative index published at the end of the year.

Women Studies Abstracts. Rush, NY: Rush Publishing
     Co., 1972- .
     Index to scholarly research on women, with
bibliographic essays, lists of special periodical
issues about women, and citations to book reviews.
Pertinent subject headings include: 'Aging,'
'Older Adults,' 'Seniors,' 'Middle Age,' 'Old Age
Survivors Insurance,' 'Senior Women.'

TOPICAL BIBLIOGRAPHIES

AGING--GENERAL

Balkema, John. A General Bibliography on Aging.
Washington, D.C.: National Council on the
Aging, 1972.
Bibliography of books published from 1967-1972.
It covers the usual range of topics in aging--the
aging process, alternatives to institutional care,
health, housing, transportation, volunteers. The
Bibliography is useful, but consult other sources
for journal articles and more recent books.

Bibliographies. Council of Planning Librarians.
1313 E. 60th Street, Chicago, IL 60637.
Over 1500 bibliographies on a wide range of
subjects. There are a number of bibliographies on
issues related to aging, some of which are listed
elsewhere in this volume. Some are annotated; most
are not. This is an excellent beginning reference.

Conrad, James H. An Annotated Bibliography of the
History of Old Age in America. Denton, TX:
Center for Studies in Aging, North Texas State
University, 1978.
List of classic and pioneering works which have
influenced modern theory and practice, drawn from
fields of history, social work, sociology,
gerontology, geriatrics, literature, and demography.
Evaluative annotations of books, journal articles,
government publications, pamphlets, dissertations,
and theses published from 1846-1977. Contains a
subject index and a chronological index.

DeLuca, Lucy. Aging: A Annotated Guide to
Government Publications. Storrs, CT:
University of Connecticut Library, 1975.
Annotations for 220 entries, published between
1960 and 1974. This publication is most useful for
historical perspective; especially valuable is the
listing of policy papers on aging.

Edwards, Willie M.; and Flynn, Frances.
Gerontology: A Core List of Significant Works.
Ann Arbor: Institute of Gerontology,
University of Michigan, 1978.
An excellent, although unannotated bibliography.
The main section lists 1,000 books, articles, con-
ferences, congresses, colloquia, and pioneering works
in the field of social gerontology.

14

Grant, Ruth. Aging Awareness: An Annotated
     Bibliography. Pittsburgh: Senior Citizen
     School Volunteer Program, Western Pennsylvania
     Gerontology Center, University of Pittsburgh,
     1979.
     A bibliography on the historical and
sociological perspectives of aging as well as
listings of literary works on aging. Can serve as
a curriculum resource guide which provides positive
images of the elderly. Interesting features
include the use of oral history in the classroom
and reviews of children's literature.

McIlvaine, B. Aging: A Guide to Reference Sources,
     Journals, and Government Publications.
     Storrs, CT: University of Connecticut Library,
     1978.
     A guide to journals, reference materials, and
government documents on the medical, social, and
economic problems of the aged. Sources published
between 1970 and 1977. The major strength of the
work is the comprehensive coverage of United States
government publications.

Moss, Walter G. Humanistic Perspectives on Aging:
     An Annotated Bibliography and Essay. Ann
     Arbor, MI: Institute of Gerontology,
     University of Michigan-Wayne State University,
     1976. 2d ed.
     Sources from the humanities which provide
insights about society's attitudes toward aging, old
age, and death.

Rooke, Mabel Leigh; and Wingrove, C. Ray.
     Gerontology: An Annotated Bibliography.
     Washington, D.C.: University Press of America,
     1977.
     Books, substantial papers, and government
documents published from 1966 to 1977 arranged into
sections on general references and 33 subject
categories, with a final section listing selected
journals and periodicals related specifically to
aging. Author index. A mixture of popular and
scholarly works.

Schwartz, Beverly. Aging Bibliography. Upper
     Montclair, NJ: National Multimedia Center for
     Adult Education, Department of Adult
     Continuing Education, Montclair State College,
     1977.
     A list of general and specialized texts,

client-use literature, instructional programs, group
leader and teaching guides, research documents,
project reports, and handbooks for program
establishment and implementation. It should be
useful for the academic community, health care
industry, and local agency or industry-based program
planner.

Simpson, Christine. "Federal Documents on Aging; A
      Selection," RQ v. 18 (Winter 1978/79), pp.
      191-196.
      A bibliographic essay describing a highly
selective number of government documents on aging
in the fields of retirement, health care, housing,
transportation, and minorities. The descriptions
are very useful for the beginning researcher.

Young, Mary E. The Elderly: Social, Health,
      Housing, and Transportation Problems and
      Services: A Bibliography with Abstracts.
      Springfield, VA: National Technical
      Information Service, 1976.
      A collection of government-sponsored research
reports dealing with senior citizens and their
problems. Contains 254 entries. The lack of
indexes reduces access to citations.

COMMUNICATION

Resource Materials for Communicative Problems of
      Older Persons. Washington, D.C.: American
      Speech and Hearing Association, 1975.
      An annotated compilation of sources on the
hearing, language, and speech problems found among
the elderly.

Sharma, Prakash C. Aging and Communication: A
      Selected Bibliographic Research Guide.
      Monticello, IL: Vance Bibliographies, 1978.
      2 vols. 225 unannotated references.
      No subject access. Dates of publication range
from 1950-1975.

DEATH AND DYING

Fulton, Robert Lester. Death, Grief, and
      Bereavement: A Bibliography, 1845-1975. New
      York: Arno, 1977.
      References to 3800 items with an empirical
perspective on topics such as the definition of
death, organ transplantation, terminal care,

euthanasia. This is one of the best bibliographies
on death and dying.

·Miller, Albert Jay. Death: A Bibliographical
     Guide. Metuchen, N.J.: Scarecrow Press, 1977.
     Selectively annotated list of books and
articles published through 1974. It is designed for
scholars, professionals, and laypeople. Subjects
included--attitudes toward death in older persons,
fear of death in the aged, nursing homes, and aged
views of death.

Poteet, G. Howard. Death and Dying: A
     Bibliography (1950-1974). Troy, N.Y.:
     Whitston, 1976.
     Attempts to be a comprehensive world-wide
bibliography for the years 1950-1974. It focuses
on the psychology of death. The bibliography is
designed for researchers in sociology, medicine,
education, and allied areas. Pertinent subject
headings--'Attitudes toward death: Geriatrics,'
'Bereavement: Widows and Widowers,' 'Care-
Geriatrics,' 'Geriatrics.'

Simpson, Michael A. Dying, Death, and Grief--A
     Critically Annotated Bibliography and Source
     Book of Thanatology and Terminal Care. New
     York: Plenum Press, 1979. 4th ed.
     Separate lists of books, journal articles,
and audio-visual sources. It is difficult to use
because indexes are not combined, but useful
because the book is so current.

                    GERIATRICS

Sharma, Prakash C. A Selected Bibliographic
     Research Guide to Geriatric Care in Advanced
     Societies. Monticello, IL: Vance
     Bibliographies, 1978.
     Useful beginning point for cross-national
comparison of policies on aging. It is divided
into a section on books and one on articles. There
is no subject access.

    HOUSING, ARCHITECTURE, ENVIRONMENTAL EFFECTS

Farber, Douglas A. Housing and Related Services
     for Exceptional Persons: A Source Book.
     Monticello, IL: Council of Planning
     Librarians, 1973.
     Essays on the aging, physically handicapped,

and mentally retarded persons followed by a
bibliography emphasizing housing and operational
aspects of program design and administration.
Published from 1960-1973. The sources listed
should be available in most university libraries.

Koncelik, Joseph A.   Considerate Design and the
     Aging: Review Article with a Selected and
     Annotated Bibliography. Monticello, IL:
     Council of Planning Librarians, 1972.
     A compilation of sources in which criteria
are established for design of products and building
interiors for the elderly.

Sharma, Prakash C. A Selected Research Guide to
     Age Segregated Housing for the Elderly Poor.
     Monticello, IL: Vance Bibliographies, 1978.
     Unannotated collection of 100 studies. It
is divided into two parts: books and articles.
No subject index, but a worthwhile starting point.

Snyder, Lorraine Hiatt. The Environmental Challenge
     and the Aging Individual. Monticello, IL:
     Council of Planning Librarians, 1972.
     A listing of reference materials emphasizing
environmental effects on older persons. Excellent
annotations.

INTERGENERATIONAL RELATIONS

Bengtson, Vern L. Intergenerational Relations and
     Aging. Los Angeles: Ethel Percy Andrus
     Gerontology Center, University of Southern
     California, 1975.
     Emphasis on English language scholarly books,
journal articles, and dissertations, published from
1950 to 1974. Contents include macro- and micro-
social analyses of generational differences,
behavior patterns, theoretical viewpoints.

MEDIA

About Aging: A Catalog of Films. Los Angeles:
     Ethel Percy Andrus Gerontology Center,
     University of Southern California, 1977.   3rd
     ed.
     Annotations of three hundred twenty-five films
in 34 categories, including some feature length and
foreign films.

Gerontological Film Collection. Denton, TX: Center

for Studies in Aging, North Texas State
University, n.d.
Listing of over 100 16mm films, filmstrips,
and slide/tape sets concerned with different aspects
of aging--attitudes toward aging, communicating with
the elderly, death, housing, sexuality, exercise,
isolation, nursing care, safety, as well as other
topics of importance.

Hollenshead, Carol. Past Sixty: The Older Woman in
Print and Film. Ann Arbor, MI: Institute of
Gerontology, University of Michigan/Wayne
State University, 1977.
Lists 289 entries for books, pamphlets, films,
and videotapes on social and psychological issues,
e.g., widowhood, sexuality, ethnic background, and
health.

Media Resources: A Comprehensive Listing. Ann
Arbor, MI: Resources in Aging, Institute of
Gerontology, University of Michigan, 1974.
A description of more than 250 films,
filmstrips, feature films, slides, transparencies,
and audio tapes relating to aging.

Neiswender, Margaret E. About Aging: A Catalog of
Films. Los Angeles: Ethel Percy Andrus
Gerontology Center, University of Southern
California, 1973.
Wide-ranging annotated list of 128 films about
aging. Each annotation includes a short
description of the content of the film, a technical
description (length, date, black and white or color),
and the source of distribution, rental and/or
purchase price.

MINORITIES

Barnes, Nell D. Black Aging: An Annotated
Bibliography. Monticello, IL: Vance
Bibliographies, 1979.
Contains references to books, journal articles,
government documents about the urban elderly as
well as the Black elderly. Coverage is from 1970-
1979. Specific subjects covered include employment,
health, education, social services, sociology,
racism, and discrimination.

Bell, Duran, and others. Delivering Services to
Elderly Members of Minority Groups: A Critical
Review of the Literature. Santa Monica, CA:

Rand, 1976.
Includes Asian and Pacific Americans, Mexican
Americans, American Indians, and Black Americans.
Following essays that provide a state-of-the art
review on research literature for each group is a
bibliography listing important research articles,
empirical studies, and models relating to social
service delivery systems.

Dancy, Joseph. The Black Elderly: A Guide for
     Practitioners with Comprehensive Bibliography.
     Ann Arbor, MI: Institute of Gerontology,
     University of Michigan-Wayne State University,
     1977.
One-third of this book is devoted to a
bibliography which serves as a guide to the
practitioner, student, and scholar. It reveals
that there is little research on (1) language and
the elderly and (2) retirement and Blacks. Topics
covered in the bibliography include demography,
family, health, nutrition, housing, income,
transportation, retirement, language, women, urban
problems.

Delgado, M. and Finley, G. E. "Spanish-speaking
     Elderly; A Bibliography," Gerontologist, 18
     (1978); 387-394.
Selected professional, research, and scholarly
references, published from 1960-1977, on the
Spanish-speaking elderly from Latin America, Spain,
and the United States. Major subject categories
include social policy issues, housing, employment,
retirement, social behavior, personality,
intellectual functioning, health, death and dying,
and demography.

Ragan, Pauline K. Black and Mexican Aging: A
     Selected Bibliography. Los Angeles: Ethel
     Percy Andrus Gerontology Center, University of
     Southern California, 1977.
A listing of books, papers, dissertations,
and government documents on the socio-cultural
aspects of aging among the Black and Mexican American
elderly. The references covering the period 1967-
1977 are partially annotated.

Suzuki, Peter T. Minority Group Aged in America: A
     Comprehensive Bibliography of Recent
     Publications on Blacks, Mexican-Americans,
     Native Americans, Chinese, and Japanese.
     Monticello, IL: Council of Planning

Librarians, 1975.

A listing of cross-cultural studies published between 1967 and 1975. This is an important summary of research for the period covered.

NUTRITION

Aging and Nutrition. Berkeley, CA: Society for Nutrition Education, 1976.

Selective listing of print and audio-visual materials from government agencies, educational and health institutions and associations, food industry and commercial sources.

Nutrition Abstracts and Reviews. See REFERENCE WORKS.

Weg, Ruth B. Nutrition and Aging: A Selected Bibliography. Los Angeles: Ethel Percy Andrus Gerontology Center, University of Southern California, 1977.

The primary focus is on the significant variables and consequences related to the adequacy and physiology of nutrition of the later years, including data from studies on affect and attitude of the elderly toward food and their eating patterns. Unannotated, covers years 1969-1977.

PSYCHOLOGY

Birren, James E. Relation of Stress and Age. Los Angeles: Ethel Percy Andrus Gerontology Center, University of Southern California, 1975.

Unannotated list of English language sources, published 1959-1974, dealing with the causes of stress and types of adjustment and maladjustment to stress.

Psychological Abstracts. See REFERENCE WORKS.

Schwartz, Arthur N. Psychological Adjustment to Aging: A Selected Bibliography. Los Angeles: Ethel Percy Andrus Gerontology Center, 1975.

Partially annotated compilation of books and journal articles published from 1959-1974. Selected contents include ego functioning, alienation, isolation and loneliness, adjustment to the climacteric, and drug abuse.

RETIREMENT, RETIREMENT INCOME, AND SOCIAL SECURITY

Hickey, Tom; and others. Retirement Planning:
    Selected References. University Park, PA:
    Gerontology Center, Institute for the Study of
    Human Development, Pennsylvania State
    University, 1975.
    A bibliography of over 1,000 scholarly and
popular books and articles on retirement and pre-
retirement planning. It also contains a list of
films, with short descriptive annotations.

Kelleher, C. H.; and Quirk, D. A. "Preparation for
    Retirement: An Annotated Bibliography of
    Literature, 1965-1974." Industrial Gerontology
    I (1974): 49-73.

Musgrave, Gerald. Social Security in the United
    States: A Classified Bibliography. Monticello,
    IL: Vance Bibliographies, 1978.
    An unannotated collection of journal articles,
books, government documents, and institute reports.
It focuses on the economic issues of social security.

RURAL AGED

Wilkinson, Carroll Wetzel. The Rural Aged in
    America, 1975-1978: An Annotated Bibliography.
    Morgantown, WV: West Virginia University,
    1978.
    A comprehensive annotated bibliography.

SAFETY

Small, Arnold M. Safety for the Elderly. Los
    Angeles: Ethel Percy Andrus Gerontology Center,
    University of Southern California, 1975.
    A listing of 300 titles on community safety,
home safety, institutional safety, physiological
research, statistics, vehicle accidents. It is a
useful compilation which is partially annotated.

SEXUALITY

Birren, James E; and Moore, Julie L. Sexuality and
    Aging: A Selected Bibliography. Los Angeles:
    Ethel Percy Andrus Gerontology Center,
    University of Southern California, 1975.
    English language sources published from 1959-
1974. The unannotated entries range from societal
aspects of sexuality and aging to the chemical

influence on sexual behavior. This is a useful
beginning, but it must be supplemented with more
recent sources.

Sha'ked, Ami. Human Sexuality in Physical and
    Mental Illnesses and Disabilities: An
    Annotated Bibliography. Bloomington, IN:
    Indiana University Press, 1978.
    Lists information regarding sexual behavior,
functioning, and difficulties associated with many
physical and mental illnesses and handicapping
conditions. It has an entire chapter on sex and the
aged.

Wharton, George F. A Bibliography on Sexuality and
    Aging. New Brunswick, NY: Intra-University
    Program in Gerontology, Rutgers University,
    1978.
    A collection of books, journal articles,
unpublished papers, and dissertations, published
during the 1960's and 1970's. Topics covered range
from the social and psychological aspects of
sexuality in the aged to chemical influence on
sexuality and the aged.

SOCIAL WORK

Carter, Beryl; and Siegel, Sheldon. An Annotated
    Selective Bibliography for Social Work with
    the Aging. New York: Council on Social Work
    Education, 1968.
    A bibliography of references covering the
methods, techniques, programs and services involved
in social service delivery to the elderly. It
lists periodical articles from 1959-1967.

Project Share. Providing Human Services to the
    Elderly. Washington, D.C.: Department of
    Health, Education, and Welfare, 1977.
    A bibliography on the delivery of social
services to the elderly. Lengthy annotations are
provided for each item. There is an author index,
but no subject approach given.

STATISTICS

Guide to Census Data on the Elderly. Washington,
    D.C.: Department of Commerce, Bureau of the
    Census, 1978.
    A description of how to find information in the
reports, computer tapes, and special tabulations

from the 1970 census which are available from the
Bureau of the Census. Especially useful for data
on ethnic groups.

Statistical Reports on Older Americans. Washington,
D.C.: Department of Health, Education, and
Welfare, Administration on Aging, Office of
Human Development, National Clearinghouse on
Aging, 1977- .
A series of reports providing statistical
information about the elderly, e.g., American
Indians, poverty among the elderly, and elderly
widows.

TRANSPORTATION

Miller, James H. A Bibliography on Transportation
for Elderly and Handicapped Persons.
Monticello, IL: Vance Bibliographies, 1978.
A compilation of government documents,
proceedings, state government publications, and
journal articles; as well as books about transportation provided by social service agencies,
accessibility to regular transit, grant programs,
and regulations. The main subject categories are
background and history, administration and planning,
transportation operational procedures, and
equipment and facilities. Although the entries are
unannotated, the bibliography is a good beginning
point.

Regnier, Victor. Mobile Services and the Elderly:
A Bibliography. Monticello, IL: Council of
Planning Librarians, 1971.
An unannotated bibliography of books and journal
articles dealing with mobile services in the
following areas: medical, dental, recreational/
cultural, commercial, social and home delivered
services, mobile service architectural design, and
transportation.

WOMEN

Edelstein, Beth; and Segedin, Liz. Age Is Becoming:
An Annotated Bibliography on Women and Aging.
Berkeley: Interface Bibliographers, 1977.
Expanded edition.
A selective bibliography of current literature
about the impact of aging on women in contemporary
America. General and scholarly publications
covering the period 1970-1977 are evaluated from a

feminist viewpoint. Topics covered include re-entry into the labor market, role changes, sexuality, physical and mental health, widowhood, biography, fiction. This is an excellent starting point for research on women and aging.

Hollenshead, Carol. Past Sixty: The Older Woman in Print and Film. See section on Media.

Strugnell, Cecile. Adjustment to Widowhood and Some Related Problems: A Selective and Annotated Bibliography. New York: Health Sciences Publishing Corporation, 1974.
     A comprehensive review of the literature on mutual help programs for widows. It is divided into topical sections such as: bereavement, widowhood, loneliness, role of women, mutual help groups.

U.S. Bureau of Labor Statistics. Where to Find BLS Statistics on Women. Washington, DC: Bureau of Labor Statistics, 1978.
     Summaries of statistics on women, especially in the field of employment, which are available from BLS. It provides information on how to acquire the data.

Women in Midlife--Security and Fulfillment. Submitted to the Select Committee on Aging and the Subcommittee on Retirement Income and Employment, U.S. House of Representatives, 95th Congress, 2d Session, Washington, DC: Government Printing Office, 1978-1979. 2 vols. vol. 1, A Compendium of Papers. vol. 2, Annotated Bibliography.
     A selectively annotated bibliography of books, journal articles, and government publications on women in midlife. The majority of the citations are from the 1970s. Subjects covered include social roles, work, education, pensions, discrimination, housing, mental health, and political participation.

Women Studies Abstracts. See REFERENCE BOOKS.

HANDBOOKS AND DIRECTORIES

Brown, Robert N. The Rights of Older Persons: The Basic ACLU Guide to an Older Person's Rights. New York: Avon, 1979.
     Outlines an individual's rights under the present law and offers suggestions on how to protect one's rights in the areas of income, health care,

freedom from restraints on life, liberty, and property.

Cohen, Lilly, and Oppedisano-Reich, Marie. A National Guide to Government and Foundation Funding Sources in the Field of Aging. Garden City, NY: Adelphi University Press, 1977.
    Arranged by subject, each entry contains objectives of the grant program, type of assistance (formula grants, contracts, research grants, scholarships, etc.), uses and restrictions, eligibility requirements, application procedures, and contact person.

Adelman, Nora E. Directory of Life Care Communities. Kennett Square, PA: Kendal-Crosslands, 1978.
    Lists 46 facilities, arranged by state. It gives name, address, sponsor, religious affiliation or management, year established or estimated completion date, type of location (rural or urban), admission requirements, current resident population, fees, and services provided.

Gerontological Society. Membership Directory. Washington, DC: the Society, 1977.
    Provides the name, type of membership, discipline, institutional affiliation, and professional function of the fellows and members of the Gerontological Society.

Norback, Craig T. The Older Americans Handbook. New York: Van Nostrand Reinhold Co., 1977.
    A directory of sources of information--where to get information, how to apply for resources, public and private agencies, state and federal agencies, associations, list of government programs, health agencies, housing, nutrition, mental health, and transportation. Good source for addresses and explanations of government programs.

Sourcebook on Aging. Chicago: Marquis Academic Media, 1977.
    A collection of essays, statistics, and excerpts, primarily from government publications. It provides a state-of-the-art overview in the field of aging, and should be useful for individuals and libraries with limited government documents collections.

Sprouse, Betsy M. National Directory of Educational Programs in Gerontology. Washington, DC:

Association for Gerontology in Higher Education,
1978.
Provides information on courses, degree
programs, financial aid for students and research
activities for 121 programs in aging. Indexed by
state.

U.S. National Clearinghouse on Aging. Thesaurus.
Washington, DC: Department of Health,
Education, and Welfare, 1977.
A listing of subject headings in the field of
gerontology.

U.S. National Institutes of Health. International
Directory of Gerontology. Washington, DC:
Government Printing Office, 1969. Biographies
of researchers in the field of gerontology.

SELECTED JOURNALS IN GERONTOLOGICAL RESEARCH

Age and Aging. London: Baillière Tindall, 1972-
quarterly.
The official journal of the British Geriatric
Society and the British Society for Research on
Aging. Indexed in Biological Abstracts, Chemical
Abstracts, Index Medicus.

Aged Care and Services Review. New York: Haworth
Press, 1978- bi-monthly. Formerly titled Aged
Care and Counseling.
A journal for mental health and health care
personnel who work with the elderly in a wide
variety of settings.

Aging International. Washington, DC: International
Federation of Aging, 1974- quarterly.
Cross-cultural data on program innovation and
service delivery, applied research, and aging policy
developments.

Aging. Washington, DC: U.S. Dept. of Health,
Education, and Welfare, Administration on
Aging, 1951- 10 issues a year.
Reports on federally funded programs on aging,
legislative actions, news of state programs. Indexed
in Index to U.S. Government Periodicals, Public
Affairs Information Service Bulletin, Readers' Guide
to Periodical Literature.

Aging and Work. Washington, DC: National Council
on the Aging, 1978- quarterly. Formerly

titled Industrial Gerontology, 1969-1977.
    References to research findings on aging in the
work force, private pension plans, employment data
by age groups, discrimination, and older worker
potentials. Indexed in Current Index to Journals in
Education, Current Contents, Excerpta Medica, Human
Resources Abstracts, Psychological Abstracts, Social
Sciences Citation Index.

American Geriatrics Society. Journal. New York:
    American Geriatrics Society, 1953- monthly.
    Articles focus on the geriatric patient.
Indexed in Biological Abstracts, Chemical Abstracts,
Hospital Literature Index, Index Medicus,
International Nursing Index, Nutrition Abstracts and
Reviews, Psychological Abstracts, Social Sciences
Citation Index.

American Society for Geriatric Dentistry. Journal.
    Chicago: American Society for Geriatric
    Dentistry, 1966- monthly.
    Indexed in Index to Dental Literature.

Dynamic Years. Washington, DC: American
    Association of Retired Persons, 1965-
    bi-monthly. Formerly titled Dynamic Maturity.
    This official publication of AARP's division,
Action for Independent Maturity, includes both
informational and entertaining articles.

Educational Gerontology. Washington, DC:
    Hemisphere Publishing Corporation, 1976-
    quarterly.
    Original papers, book, and subject reviews on
adult education. It includes a list of books and
government documents on all aspects of gerontology.
Indexed in Current Index to Journals in Education,
Psychological Abstracts.

Experimental Aging Research. Bar Harbor, ME:
    Experimental Aging, Research, Inc., 1975-
    bi-monthly.
    An international, interdisciplinary journal
dealing with the process of aging and the aged in
humans and animals. Indexed in Biological Abstracts,
Index Medicus, Psychological Abstracts.

Experimental Gerontology. Elmsford, NY: Pergamon
    Press, 1964- bi-monthly.
    An international scholarly journal primarily
directed to the doctor or health care professional.

Indexed in Biological Abstracts, Chemical Abstracts, Index Medicus, Social Sciences Citation Index.

Geriatrics. Minneapolis, MN: American Geriatrics
    Society, 1946- monthly.
    Emphasis on the physiological and psychological aspects of the aging process and care of aged patients. Indexed in Biological Abstracts, Chemical Abstracts, Index Medicus, Psychological Abstracts.

The Gerontologist. Washington, DC: Gerontological
    Society, 1961- bi-monthly.
    Articles on social policy, historical analysis, theory, research, book reviews, and new developments in gerontology. Indexed in Biological Abstracts, Chemical Abstracts, Hospital Literature Index, Index Medicus, International Nursing Index, Psychological Abstracts, Social Sciences Citation Index, Sociological Abstracts, Social Sciences Index.

Gerontology. Basel, Switzerland. S. Karger, 1976-
    bi-monthly.
    An international journal of experimental and clinical gerontology formed by the union of Gerontologia and Gerontologia Clinica. Indexed in Biological Abstracts, Chemical Abstracts, Index Medicus.

International Journal of Aging and Human
    Development. Farmingdale, NY: Baywood
    Publishing Co., 1973- quarterly. Formerly
    titled Aging and Human Development.
    Emphasizes psychosocial gerontology. Indexed in Index Medicus, Psychological Abstracts, Social Sciences Citation Index.

Journal of Geriatric Psychiatry. New York:
    International Universities Press, 1967- semi-
    annual.
    Official journal of the Boston Society for Gerontological Psychiatry. Includes recent findings and new information in geriatric psychiatry. Indexed in Index Medicus, Psychological Abstracts, Social Sciences Citation Index.

Journal of Gerontological Nursing. Thorofare, NJ:
    Charles B. Slack Publications, 1975-
    bi-monthly.
    Theory and methodology of geriatric nursing. Indexed in Cumulative Index to Nursing Literature, International Nursing Index.

Journal of Gerontological Social Work. New York:
     Haworth Press, 1978- quarterly.
     Indexed in Psychological Abstracts, Sociologi-
cal Abstracts.

Journal of Gerontology. Washington, DC:
     Gerontological Society, 1946- bi-monthly.
     Includes articles on biological and medical
sciences, psychology and social sciences, social
gerontology, book reviews, and a list of current
publications. Indexed in Biological Abstracts,
Chemical Abstracts, Index Medicus, Hospital
Literature Index, Nuclear Science Abstracts,
Nutrition Abstracts and Reviews, Public Affairs
Information Service Bulletin, Social Sciences
Citation Index.

Journal of Minority Aging. Durham, NC: National
     Council on Black Aging, 1975- quarterly.
     Formerly titled Black Aging.
     Addresses the problems of being old and black
in America from social, cultural, and political
viewpoints.

Mechanisms of Ageing and Development. Lausanne,
     Switzerland: Elsevier Sequoia S.A., 1972-
     bi-monthly.
     Indexed in Biological Abstracts, Chemical
Abstracts, Current Contents, Excerpta Medica, Index
Medicus, Science Citation Index.

Modern Maturity. Washington, DC: American
     Association of Retired Persons, 1958-
     bi-monthly.
     Social welfare, education, health, political
developments are areas emphasized in this official
journal of AARP.

Omega: The Journal of Death and Dying.
     Farmingdale, NY: Baywood Publishing, 1970-
     quarterly.
     Psychological studies on dying, death, grief,
suicide and behavioral effects among all age groups.
Indexed in Biological Abstracts, Excerpta Medica,
Psychological Abstracts.

Perspective on Aging. Washington, DC: National
     Council on the Aging, 1972- bi-monthly.
     Reports of activities of older persons, federal
programs, book reviews, public policy developments,
and council activities.

Research on Aging. Beverly Hills, CA: Sage
     Publications, 1979- quarterly.

Senior Citizen News. Washington, DC: National
     Council of Senior Citizens, 1973- monthly.
     Bulletin of legislative activities.

Social Security Bulletin. Washington, DC:
     Government Printing Office, 1938- monthly.
     Studies of federal legislation, programs,
research, and statistical information on social
security. Indexed in Business Periodicals Index,
Public Affairs Information Service Bulletin, Social
Sciences Citation Index, Index to U.S. Government
Periodicals.

ASSOCIATIONS IN GERONTOLOGY

Action for Independent Maturity. 1909 K Street,
     N.W., Washington, DC 20049. Division of the
     American Association of Retired Persons.
     Helps people in mid-life prepare for retirement
and to reach the full limit of their potential
through more effective use of their time, money,
and energy. Publishes Dynamic Years, Aim Action,
and Retirement Planning Handbook.

American Association for Geriatric Psychiatry. 230
     N. Michigan Ave., Suite 2400, Chicago, IL
     60601.
     Psychiatrists interested in promoting better
mental health care for the elderly. Publishes
Newsletter.

American Association of Homes for the Aging. 1050
     17th Street, N.W., Washington, DC 20036.
     Members are voluntary, non-profit, and
governmental homes for the aging as well as
interested individuals and organizations. Develops
curricula for administrators of homes, conducts
institutes and workshops on current concerns.
Publishes Washington Report, Housing Report, Legal
Report, Association Report, Directory of
Consultants-Planning Housing for the Elderly, and
Directory of Nonprofit Homes for the Aged-Social
Components of Care.

American Association of Retired Persons. 1909 K
     Street, N.W., Washington, DC 20049.
     For persons 55 years of age or older, whether
or not retired. Purpose is to improve every aspect

of living for older people. Affiliated with National
Retired Teachers Association. Publishes News
Bulletin, Modern Maturity.

American Geriatrics Society. 10 Columbus Circle,
        New York, NY 10019.
        Professional society of physicians interested
in problems of the aged. Publishes Journal of the
AGS, Newsletter, Clinical Aspects of the Aging
(book).

Association for Gerontology in Higher Education.
        1835 K Street, N.W., Suite 305, Washington, DC.
        Promotes and encourages education and training
of persons preparing for research or careers in
gerontology and increases public awareness of the
needs of such training. Publishes Newsletter,
Gerontology in Higher Education, National Directory
of Educational Programs in Gerontology.

Association for Humanistic Gerontology. 1711 Solano
        Avenue, Berkeley, CA 94707.
        Serves as international resource sharing network
and as an information clearinghouse. Publishes
Newsletter, Journal of Humanistic Gerontology.

Gerontological Society. 1835 K Street, N.W., Suite
        305, Washington, DC 20006.
        Promotes scientific study of the aging process
and publishes information about aging. Publishes
The Gerontologist, Journal of Gerontology.

Gray Panthers. 3700 Chestnut Street, Philadelphia,
        PA 19104.
        Consciousness-raising activist group of older
adults (over 65) and young people. Combats ageism.
Advises, acts as a catalyst, organizes local groups
of young and old who work on issues of their own
choice. Maintains information and referral service.
Publishes The Network Newspaper.

International Association of Gerontology. c/o Tokyo
        Metropolitan Geriatric Hospital, Itabashiku,
        Tokyo 173, Japan.
        Promotes gerontological research in each of the
biological, medical, and social fields, carried out
by gerontological associations, societies or groups;
promotes cooperation among the members of these
associations; and promotes training of personnel in
the field of aging. Publishes IAG news in The
Gerontologist.

International Federation on Ageing. 1909 K Street,
    N.W., Washington, DC   20049.
    Federation of voluntary organizations from 26
countries that represent the elderly as their
advocates and/or provide services to them. Serves
as an international advocate for the aging;
exchanges information on a cross-national level of
developments in aging; assists in the creation of
associations of the aging; sponsors conferences and
symposia. Publishes Ageing International.

National Alliance of Senior Citizens. 777 14th
    Street, N.W., Washington, DC   20005.
    Purpose is to inform the membership and the
American public of the needs of senior citizens
and of the programs and policies available from
government and other groups. Maintains Golden Age
Hall of Fame. Publishes The Senior Independent,
Senior Services Manual.

National Association of Area Agencies on Aging.
    1828 L Street, N.W., Washington, DC   20036.
    Members are Area Agencies on Aging. Goals are
the development of a national policy on aging,
communication within the national network on aging
(composed of the Administration on Aging, state
units on aging, and area agencies on aging).
Publishes The Point of Delivery.

National Association of Older Americans. 12 Electric
    Street, West Alexandria, OH   45381.
    Purpose is to reestablish a satisfactory level
of comfort and security for older Americans, restore
a dignity to the image of the elderly, and provide
individual assistance and information to older
Americans.   Publishes The Heartline/NAOA Newsletter.

National Association of State Units on Aging. 1828
    L Street, Suite 400, Washington, DC   20036.
    National coordination mechanism for state
agencies on aging. Collects, analyzes and
disseminates information relating to the operation
of state agencies on aging. Publishes Bulletin,
Memos.

National Council on the Aging. 1828 L Street, N.W.,
    Washington, DC   20036.
    Works with and through other organizations to
develop concern for older people, as well as methods
and resources for meeting their needs. Provides a
national information and consultation center, holds

conferences and workshops, conducts research and
demonstration programs on various problems of older
people. Publishes Newsletter, Perspective on Aging,
Aging and Work, Current Literature on Aging.

National Council on Black Aging. Box 8813, Durham,
      NC 27707.
      Persons interested in policies affecting aged
blacks and the dissemination of research.
Publishes Journal of Minority Aging.

National Council of Senior Citizens. 1511 K Street,
      N.W., Washington, DC 20005.
      Organization of 3800 autonomous senior citizens
clubs, associations, councils, and other groups with
a combined membership of over 3,000,000 persons.
Educational and action group; sponsors mass rallies,
educational workshops and leadership training
institutes; distributes films, news releases, and
special reports. Publishes Senior Citizens News.

National Geriatrics Society. 212 W. Wisconsin Ave.,
      Third Floor, Milwaukee, WI 53203.
      Promotes maintenance of proper operational
standards and qualified administration of facilities
caring for the aged. Publishes Aging and Leisure
Living, News, Nursing Care Requirements in the
States of the Union.

National Retired Teachers Association. 1909 K
      Street, N.W., Washington, DC 20049.
      Provides social services for retired teachers,
e.g., group insurance. Sponsors competitions, awards,
speakers bureau. Compiles statistics. Affiliated
with American Association of Retired Persons,
International Federation on Ageing. Publishes News
Bulletin, Journal.

Urban Elderly Coalition. 1828 L Street, N.W.,
      Suite 505, Washington, DC 20036.
      Objectives are to develop workable solutions
to the special needs of the urban elderly, to
analyze and inform about legislation affecting the
elderly, to exchange technical information about
and among the urban aging programs, to mobilize
support of state and federal governments, to build
a coherent and strong national association of urban
leaders on aging. Affiliated with Ad Hoc Coalition
on National Council on Aging. Publishes Legislative
Update, Technical Exchange Bulletin, position papers.

SELECTED UNITED STATES GOVERNMENT AGENCIES
AND PROGRAMS IN GERONTOLOGY

Administration on Aging.
    The principal federal organization for
identifying the needs, concerns, and interests of
older persons and for carrying out the programs of
the Older Americans Act. It administers a program
of formula grants to state agencies on aging to
serve as advocates for the elderly and to assist
in the establishment of comprehensive, coordinated
service systems for older persons at the community
level. AOA awards grants for research,
demonstrations, and manpower development projects.

Foster Grandparent Program.
    Created in 1965, the program offers to men and
women over 60 the opportunity to work in schools
and hospitals for retarded, disturbed, and handicapped children in day care centers, city hospital
wards, correctional institutions, homes for
disadvantaged, dependent, or neglected children,
and other settings within the community.

Independent Living for the Disabled.
    Department-wide functions for the Department of
Housing and Urban Development programs for housing,
community, and neighborhood development, and related
facilities and services for disabled persons.

Medicare.
    Provides basic health benefits to recipients of
social security.

Retired Senior Volunteer Program (RSVP).
    Persons of retirement age perform volunteer
services according to community needs in a variety
of settings, including schools, courts, health care,
rehabilitation, day care, youth and other community
centers.

Senior Companion Program.
    Provides part-time, volunteer opportunities
for low-income older persons. The volunteer offers
person-to-person services to adults with special
needs in a variety of settings--hospitals,
institutions for the physically, emotionally, or
mentally handicapped, correctional facilities,
senior day-care settings, and private homes.

Senior Community Service Employment Program.
    Makes subsidized, part-time job opportunities in community service activities available to low-income persons aged 55 and above.

Social Security Administration.
    Principal functions include research and recommendations on the problems of poverty, insecurity, and health care for the aged, blind, and disabled; and policy guidance for the administration of the retirement, survivors, and disability insurance programs, as well as the supplemental security income program.

2
General Perspectives on Aging

The following list identifies a number of basic
books and articles in the field of gerontology,
particularly social gerontology. Some are classics,
representing major theoretical positions or the
results of an important study. There are a number
of standard reference volumes--compendiums of
articles by important writers in the field. Other,
more recent works, provide a historical perspective.
Several volumes are statements by the aged
themselves. This list also identifies a few of the
better anthologies--collections of significant
previously published writings in the field. Taken
as a whole, these writings should provide a solid
grounding for anyone seriously interested in the
study of aging.

GENERAL WORKS: ANNOTATED REFERENCES

BOOKS

Achenbaum, Andrew; and Kusnerz, Peggy Ann. <u>Images
of Old Age in America: 1790 to the Present.</u>
Ann Arbor, MI: Institute of Gerontology, The
University of Michigan-Wayne State University,
1978.
An examination of historical and contemporary
pictorial images of American old people. The
commentary is very brief; there is something of a
"coffee table book" format to the volume. The
images have been arranged in historical order and
are analyzed in terms of the themes developed by
Achenbaum in <u>Old Age in the New Land</u>.

Achenbaum, Andrew. <u>Old Age in the New Land: The
   American Experience Since 1790</u>. Baltimore:
   Johns Hopkins University Press, 1978.
   A comprehensive historical analysis of
society's perceptions and treatment of the aged.
Achenbaum uses modernization theory to provide
perspective for a large body of social, cultural,
and historical data. The documentation and
bibliographical notes are excellent.

Atchley, Robert C. <u>The Social Forces in Later Life:
   An Introduction to Social Gerontology</u>. Belmont,
   CA: Wadsworth, 3rd ed., 1980.
   An interdisciplinary approach to the field
designed as a text for upper level undergraduates
and beginning graduate students. This is one of
the better books of its kind. Theoretical
discussions are illustrated with research data.
There is a useful appendix on methodology, and an
outstanding bibliography which stresses periodical
literature.

Barry, John R.; and Wingrove, C. Ray, editors.
   <u>Let's Learn About Aging: A Book of Readings</u>.
   New York: John Wiley and Sons, 1977.
   An excellent reader providing a broad overview
of the field. A number of "classic" articles from
scholarly journals and some popular magazines, as
well as a few original essays and previously
unpublished papers are included. The articles
often feature useful critiques and explanations
of current theory and methodology. It is designed
for the undergraduate and general audience.

de Beauvoir, Simone. <u>The Coming of Age</u>. translated
   by Patrick O'Brien. New York: Putnam, 1972.
   A famous volume by the novelist and essayist.
She has drawn on vast literary sources to create a
portrait of the aged--and their place in society--
throughout history. The book is polemical, intended
as an indictment of society's treatment of the
elderly.

Bell, Bill, editor. <u>Contemporary Social Gerontology:
   Significant Developments in the Field of Aging</u>.
   Springfield, IL: Charles C. Thomas, 1976.
   A reader, featuring reprints of significant
articles in social gerontology. The author provides
useful introductions to each section.

Berghorn, Forrest J.; Schafer, Donna E.; and
    Associates. The Dynamics of Aging. Boulder,
    CO: Westview Press (forthcoming, summer, 1980).
    An interdisciplinary collection of original
essays that examine many aspects of growing old:
physical and mental changes, demographics, economics,
politics, death and dying, quality of life,
environments, ethnicity, sexuality, and
intergenerational and family relations. In addition
to the scholarly chapters that comprise the majority
of the volume, a special feature is the inclusion
of short pieces by service professionals working in
the field.

Bier, William C., editor. Aging: Its Challenge to
    the Individual and to Society. New York:
    Fordham University Press, 1974.
    A volume produced by the Pastoral Psychology
Institute at Fordham. It is interdisciplinary with
special attention given to religious issues as
related to aging. Other focuses are history,
psychology, physiology, retirement, and services.

Binstock, Robert H.; and Shanas, Ethel. Handbook of
    Aging and the Social Sciences. New York: Van
    Nostrand Reinhold Co., 1976.
    Currently the major collection of essays in
social gerontology. This volume is one of three;
the others focus on biological and psychological
aging. There are particularly useful studies of the
historical circumstances of the aged, family
patterns, support networks, and status and role
changes. All the Handbooks feature some of the best
known researchers in gerontology, and all have
excellent bibliographical listings. These books
are designed for the advanced student and researcher,
but some articles should be useful to the less
sophisticated reader.

Birren, James E., editor. Handbook of Aging and the
    Individual: Psychological and Biological
    Aspects. Chicago: University of Chicago
    Press, 1959.
    An earlier work, not part of the series noted
above. This volume is intended for graduate
students and professionals, but, as with most such
compendiums, some essays will be quite helpful to
more general readers. The book is divided into four
sections: Foundations of Research on Aging,
Biological Bases of Aging, Aging in Environmental
Settings, and Psychological Characteristics of

Aging. The discussions focus on history, theory,
and methodology.

Birren, James E.; and Schaie, K. Warner, editors.
    Handbook of the Psychology of Aging. New York:
    Van Nostrand Reinhold, 1977.
    (See Psychology section). The companion volume
to Binstock and Shanas, above.

Blau, Zena Smith. Old Age in a Changing Society.
    New York: Franklin Watts, 1973.
    A collection of essays by a sociologist. The
general theme is that of role loss, and there are
discussions of the aged and their children,
friendships, illness and work, and role change.
Included is the previously published, well-known
essay, "Structural Constraints on Friendship."

Brown, Mollie, editor. Readings in Gerontology.
    St. Louis: C. V. Mosby, 1978, 2nd edition.
    A short useful reader that includes previously
published articles plus four original pieces.
Brown is a nurse, and the book tends to be somewhat
oriented to medical, physiological, and psychological questions, although there are social gerontological articles as well. The essays are clearly
written and should be useful to the beginning
student.

Burgess, Ernest, editor. Aging in Western Societies.
    Chicago: University of Chicago Press, 1960.
    A companion volume to Birren, 1959, above.
This volume considers aging in a cross-cultural
perspective. Although now somewhat dated, it was
an important early effort to consider aging in the
light of cultural influence.

Butler, Robert N. Why Survive? Being Old in
    America. New York: Harper and Row, 1975.
    Butler, the first director of the National
Institute of Aging, won a Pulitzer Prize for this
popular presentation of the status of the aged in
our society. His opening line sets the tone: "Old
age in America is often a tragedy." The book is an
often angry exposé of current practices and
attitudes. It is carefully documented, and there
are excellent appendices on literature and
organizations related to the elderly.

Comfort, Alex. A Good Age. New York: Simon and
    Schuster, 1976.

A volume for the general audience designed to refute negative myths and stereotypes about the aged. Like Butler, Comfort is a prominent physician specializing in the needs and care of older people. This volume uses lucid, non-technical prose to present information from a wide range of fields. Excellent graphics, literary excerpts and biographical vignettes contribute to the positive, upbeat message.

Cumming, Elaine; and Henry, Will. Growing Old: The Process of Disengagement. New York: Basic Books, 1961.
A classic theoretical work in gerontological history. The authors interpreted findings from a Kansas City study as indicating that in order to age successfully, an older person must gradually withdraw or "disengage" from the roles and activities of earlier years. The argument had enormous impact at the time. Although the theory is now widely disputed, most researchers have felt compelled to respond to it in some way in their own work.

Curtin, Sharon R. Nobody Ever Died of Old Age. Boston: Little, Brown, 1972.
A "manifesto" protesting society's treatment of the aged. Curtin, a nurse, uses personal experiences to argue that old age should be as rewarding as other stages of life. The writing is clear; the portraits of the elderly are vivid. This book was widely acclaimed at the time of publication and it remains an important and often moving statement.

Finch, Caleb; and Hayflick, Leonard, editors. Handbook of the Biology of Aging. New York: Van Nostrand Reinhold, 1977.
The companion volume to Binstock and Shanas, and Birren and Schaie, above. (See Physiology/ Biology section).

Fischer, David H. Growing Old in America. New York: Oxford University Press, 1978.
An historical account of attitudes toward and treatment of the aged in American society. Fischer argues that the veneration and respect accorded the aged in early American society gave way to a "cult of youth" which displaced the elderly. Old age gradually came to be perceived as a social problem, giving rise to a complex system of institutional and social supports. The author has surveyed a vast

amount of material, and arrived at a somewhat
different interpretation than Achenbaum.

Fontana, Andrea. The Last Frontier: The Social
    Meaning of Growing Old. Beverly Hills: Sage
    Publications/Library of Social Research, 1977.
    A theoretical piece based on fieldwork in
several retirement settings. The author reviews
the major theories in gerontology, and then suggests
that a theory of leisure is most appropriate to
understanding the aging process. The summaries of
the theories are clear and helpful; this is a
well-written, engaging volume suitable for all
levels of gerontological study.

Gold, Don. Until the Singing Stops: A Celebration
    of Life and Old Age in America. New York:
    Holt, Rinehart and Winston, 1979.
    An oral history of people over age sixty-five
who have led "positive lives." While this is not
a scholarly work, it is an appealing volume that
suggests the great diversity of experiences and
circumstances of those who age successfully.

Gubrium, Jaber F., editor. Time, Roles, and Self in
    Old Age. New York: Human Sciences Press/
    Behavioral Publications, 1976.
    A collection of papers that address the
question of the roles held by the elderly in various
social arrangements. There are discussions of
disengagement, the politics of age, widowhood, roles
of women, the generation gap, and intergenerational
relationships.

Harris, Louis, and Associates, Inc. The Myth and
    Reality of Aging in America. Washington, DC:
    National Council on the Aging, 1975.
    The summary report of a national survey,
conducted in 1974, to determine the attitudes of the
American public toward old age. It also records
attitudes and experiences of old people themselves.
Findings revealed that older people wished to remain
active and involved, that they frequently perceived
themselves as being better off than commonly assumed
by the general public, and that they believed that
social support should increase with inflation. The
sample was disaggregated according to age and race.
This is a frequently cited survey that touches on a
broad range of issues.

Hendricks, Jon; and Hendricks, C. Davis. Aging in
    Mass Society: Myths and Realities. Cambridge,
    MA: Winthrop Publishers, 1977.
    A very good, upper level text that provides a
broad interdisciplinary perspective on the field.
Excellent bibliographics accompany each chapter.

Hess, Beth, editor. Growing Old in America. New
    Brunswick, NJ: Transaction Books, 1976.
    A social gerontology reader that includes a
number of articles previously published in the
Gerontologist. There are no physiological/biological
articles. Unlike many anthologies, there are
several good historical essays. Other articles
focus on middle age, bereavement, retirement and
family life.

Hessel, Dieter, editor. Maggie Kuhn on Aging: A
    Dialogue. Philadelphia: Westminster Press,
    1977.
    The views of the founder of the Gray Panthers
as expressed during a week long Pastoral Studies
Program. A wide range of old age issues are
considered from a religious and church-related
perspective.

Hoffman, Adeline, editor. The Daily Needs and
    Interests of Older People. Springfield, IL:
    Charles C. Thomas, 1970.
    A collection of essays intended for home
economists and other service workers with
responsibilities to the elderly. It is a good
interdisciplinary volume that should be useful to
most students. Articles by prominent writers
discuss politics, economics, psychological concerns,
leisure, religion, biological changes, nutrition,
housing, clothing, family relations, community
services, etc.

Jenkins, Sara. Past, Present: Recording Life
    Stories of Older People. St. Alban's Parish,
    Washington, DC: National Council on Aging,
    1978.
    A short manual for conducting oral histories
with older people. The book includes examples from
interviews, and provides careful instructions for
conducting an oral history project.

Kalish, Richard A. The Later Years: Social
    Applications of Gerontology. Monterey, CA:
    Brooks/Cole, 1977.

An interdisciplinary reader comprised for the
most part of reprinted pieces from a wide range of
sources. The book is oriented somewhat to service
providers and planners, but should be quite useful
to the general reader. The focus is on the
circumstances of being old, rather than theory and
methodology. Topics included are: demographic
profiles, psychosocial aspects, economics,
retirement, health and illness, politics and law,
social institutions, the environment, social
services and institutionalization.

Kart, Cary; and Manard, Barbara, editors. Aging in
     America: Readings in Social Gerontology. New
     York: Alfred Publishing, 1976.
     A good anthology that includes many well-known,
previously published articles. Topics covered
include: theory and methodology; biological and
psychological aspects; work, retirement and leisure;
environments; institutionalization; and death and
dying.

Kimmel, Douglas C. Adulthood and Aging: An
     Interdisciplinary Developmental View. New York:
     John Wiley and Sons, 1974.
     An interdisciplinary volume that uses six case
studies to demonstrate the interrelationship of
psychological, social, and physiological factors.
The author writes from a developmental perspective,
and begins with his work with young adulthood. This
is a basic book, designed for the beginning or
general student. He does a good job of presenting
important studies and researchers in the field.

Neugarten, Bernice, editor. Middle Age and Aging:
     A Reader in Social Psychology. Chicago:
     University of Chicago Press, 1968.
     One of the major anthologies in the field.
According to the editor, the "emphasis in this
volume is upon social and psychological processes
as individuals move from middle age to old age.
The selections represent some of the major topics
that lie closest to the question. . . ." The book
is intended for the graduate student. It includes
many empirical studies as well as theoretical
pieces. Some of the general topics are: age
status and age-sex roles; psychological changes in
the life cycle; social-psychological theories of
aging; social psychology of health; family
relationships; work, leisure, and retirement; social
environment; cross-cultural comparisons; and time,

dying, and death. The emphasis throughout is on
"normal" rather than pathological aging.

Proceedings of the Annual Southern Conference on
     Gerontology. Gainesville, FL: University of
     Florida Press, annual publication since 1951.
     Edited monographs that include the papers
presented at the annual conference. Each conference
addresses a particular theme, e.g. retirement,
health, planning, migration, etc. The monographs
are of mixed quality; some are excellent, some are
now quite dated.

Puner, Morton. To the Good Long Life: What We Know
     About Growing Old. New York: Universe Books,
     1975.
     A monograph that presents an interdisciplinary
perspective on aging. The tone is upbeat, with
numerous examples of successful aging. This is a
clearly written introductory work that incorporates
many of the major ideas current in gerontology.

Rose, Arnold M.; and Peterson, Warren A., editors.
     Older People and Their Social World.
     Philadelphia, PA: F. A. Davis, 1965.
     A volume of articles based on research on the
aging conducted in the Midwest. The essays are
useful as examples of different theoretical and
methodological approaches. Much of the research was
conducted among old people in community settings,
although there are also discussions of the
institutionalized elderly. One of the articles is
Rose's often cited "Subculture of Aging."

Rosow, Irving. Social Integration of the Aged.
     NY: The Free Press, 1967.
     A significant book that reports on a study of
friendship among the aged living in apartment
buildings in Cleveland. Rosow found that old people
living in neighborhoods with highly age-concentrated
populations were more likely to form friendships,
and to form them with age peers, than were old
people living in less concentrated neighborhoods.
There were class differences in friendship formation.
An important dimension of his analysis was the
level of morale experienced by residents of the
different neighborhoods.

_____. Socialization to Old Age. Berkeley:
     University of California Press, 1974.
     An important theoretical work that views old

age as a change in status and argues that "unlike
earlier status changes in American life, people are
not effectively socialized to old age." There is a
general lack of norms for old age, and people
consequently do not have clear expectations for the
roles they are to assume.

Saul, Shura. <u>Aging: An Album of People Growing
Old</u>. NY: John Wiley and Sons, 1974.
An anthology of anecdotes and vignettes
intended to sensitize service providers who work
with the elderly. The older people described in the
book are usually urban, from the lower and lower-
middle classes. The book is designed for classroom
use and concludes with a section on implications for
service and teaching. It is characterized by a
personal and emotional tone.

Scott-Maxwell, Florida. <u>The Measure of My Days</u>.
London: Stuart and Watkins, 1968.
One of the better known "what it's like to be
old" books. Scott-Maxwell's sensitive reflections
touch on many aspects of aging and range from the
humorous to the profound.

Shanas, Ethel; Townsend, Peter; Wedderburn, Dorothy;
Friis, Henning; Milhoj, Paul; and Stehouwer,
Jan. <u>Old People in Three Industrial Societies</u>.
NY: Atherton Press, 1968.
The report of a cross-national survey conducted
in 1962 in Denmark, Britain, and the United States.
The researchers considered such questions as health,
psychology, services, family structure and
relations, work and retirement and financial
resources. Their conclusion was significant: "old
people are more integrated in industrial society
than usually assumed, but . . . certain aspects of
social structure and organization serve to keep old
people at a distance."

_____, editor. <u>Aging in Contemporary Society</u>.
Beverly Hills: Sage Publications, 1970.
A short volume that originally appeared as a
special issue of <u>American Behavioral Scientist</u>
(14:1, 1970). The articles have a social and
cultural emphasis: family, widowhood, friends and
neighbors, work and economics, politics, and some
cross-cultural comparisons.

Spicker, Stuart F.; Woodward, Kathleen; Van Tassel,
David D., editors. <u>Aging and the Elderly</u>:

Humanistic Perspectives in Gerontology.
Atlantic Highlands, NJ: Humanities Press, 1978.
A volume of original essays on humanistic
sources for the study of aging. The authors
consider various themes (e.g. modernization, death
and dying) related to aging, and support their
discussions with examples from art, literature,
history, and philosophy.

Stearns, Peter N. Old Age in European Society: The
Case of France. London: Croom Helm, 1977.
An historical study that examines the impact
on old people as France evolved from a traditional
to a modern society. The author uses a number of
measures by which to assess the change, and offers
some stimulating theoretical discussions.

Tibbitts, Clark, editor. Handbook of Social
Gerontology: Societal Aspects of Aging.
Chicago Press, 1960.
A companion volume to Birren's Handbook, and
Burgess' Aging in Western Societies. Together, the
three volumes represented the major comprehensive
reference works of their day. The original essays
were supposed to present a conceptual framework,
review relevant research, and make suggestions for
future research. Although the volume is now
somewhat dated, many of the articles remain useful,
addressing such topics as aging in pre-industrial
societies, politics, religion, voluntary
associations, family relationships, etc.

Tunstall, Jeremy. Old and Alone: A Sociological
Study of Old People. London: Routledge and
Kegan Paul, 1966.
A British study based on surveys done in 1962.
The subjects were old people living in private
households. Interviews are interspersed among
chapters dealing with older peoples' use of time and
money, social relations, and personality. The
author proposes four categories of being alone.

U.S. Department of Health, Education and Welfare,
Office of Human Development, Administration on
Aging. Older Americans Act of 1965, As Amended,
and Related Acts. March, 1976.
The comprehensive aging legislation that created
the Administration on Aging, gerontology centers,
senior centers, and nutrition programs.

Watson, Wilbur H.; and Maxwell, Robert J., editors.
Human Aging and Dying: A Study in Sociocultural
Gerontology. New York: St. Martin's Press,
1977.
A series of studies that present cultural and
institutional variations in aging and dying. The
authors attempt to determine what enhances or
demeans the status of the aged as they examine, for
example, the residents of a Jewish home for the aged
in one study and residents of a Black old age home
in another. Various theoretical and methodological
perspectives are presented. This volume will
probably be most useful to the more advanced student.

Woodruff, Diana S.; and Birren, James E., editors.
Aging: Scientific Perspectives and Social
Issues. New York: D. Van Nostrand, 1975.
An interdisciplinary collection of original
articles that cover the full range of aging-related
issues. This is an excellent volume, perhaps best
suited for upper level undergraduates and beginning
graduate students.

Youmans, E. Grant, editor. Older Rural Americans:
A Sociological Perspective. Lexington, KY:
University of Kentucky Press, 1967.
One of the few works to consider the diverse
nature of the rural elderly population. Articles
focus on social, demographic, economic, housing
and health issues, as well as ethnic minorities.

GENERAL WORKS: OTHER REFERENCES

BOOKS

Berghorn, Forrest J.; Schafer, Donna E.; Steere,
Geoffrey; and Wiseman, Robert. The Urban
Elderly: A Study in Life Satisfaction. New
York: Allenheld Osmun/Universe Books, 1978.

Donahue, Wilma; Tibbitts, Clark; and Williams,
Richard, editors. Social and Psychological
Processes of Aging. New York: Atherton Press,
1963.

Foner, Anne, special editor. American Behavioral
Scientist 19:2 (1975). Special aging issue.

Hershey, Daniel. Lifespan and Factors Affecting It:
Aging Theories in Gerontology. Springfield,
IL: Charles C. Thomas, 1974.

Hobman, David, editor. The Social Challenge of
    Ageing. London: Croom Helm, 1978.

Kaplan, Max. Leisure: Lifestyle and Lifespan--
    Perspectives for Gerontology. Philadelphia:
    W. B. Saunders, 1979.

Kent, Donald P.; Kastenbaum, Robert; and Sherwood,
    Sylvia, editors. Research Planning and Action
    for the Elderly. New York: Behavioral
    Publications, 1972.

Kleemeier, Robert W., editor. Aging and Leisure:
    A Research Perspective Into the Meaningful
    Use of Time. New York: Oxford University
    Press, 1961.

McKinney, John; and de Vyver, Frank T., editors.
    Aging and Social Policy. New York: Appleton-
    Century-Crofts, 1966.

Palmore, Erdman B., editor. Normal Aging: Reports
    from the Duke Longitudinal Study, 1955-1969.
    Durham, NC: Duke University Press, 1970.

_____, editor. Normal Aging II: Report from the
    Duke Longitudinal Studies, 1970-1973. Durham,
    NC: Duke University Press, 1974.

Pfeiffer, Eric, editor. Successful Aging: A
    Conference Report. Durham, NC: Center for the
    Study of Aging and Human Development, Duke
    University, 1974.

Riley, Matilda White, editor. Aging from Birth to
    Death: Interdisciplinary Perspectives.
    Boulder, CO: Westview Press, 1979.

_____; and Foner, Anne. Aging and Society, V. 1:
    An Inventory of Research Findings. New York:
    Russell Sage Foundation, 1968.

_____; Riley, John W. Jr.; and Johnson, Marilyn
    E., editors. Aging and Society, V. 2: Aging
    and the Professions. New York: Russell Sage
    Foundation, 1969.

_____; Johnson, Marilyn E.; and Foner, Anne.
    Aging and Society, V. 3: A Sociology of Age
    Stratification. New York: Russell Sage
    Foundation, 1972.

50

Seltzer, Mildred M.; Corbett, Sherry L.; and Atchley,
Robert C., editors. Social Problems of the
Aging: Readings. Belmont, CA: Wadsworth,
1978.

Simpson, Ida Harper; and McKinney, John C., editors.
Social Aspects of Aging. Durham, NC: Duke
University Press, 1966.

Tibbitts, Clark; Donahue, Wilma, editors. Social
and Psychological Aspects of Aging. New York:
Columbia University Press, 1962.

_____, editors. Aging in Today's Society.
Englewood Cliffs, NJ: Prentice-Hall, 1960.

Vedder, Clyde B., editor. Gerontology: A Book of
Readings. Springfield, IL: Charles C. Thomas,
1963.

Williams, Richard H.; Tibbits, Clark; and Donahue,
Wilma, editors. Process of Aging: Social and
Psychological Perspectives. New York: Atherton
Press, 1963.

_____; and Wirths, Claudine G. Lives Through the
Years: Styles of Life and Successful Aging.
New York: Atherton Press, 1965.

ARTICLES

The following is a brief list of articles that
present some of the various theoretical positions
in social gerontology. A number of the selections
are included in the works listed above; they are
identified here in order to provide an introduction
to some of the basic arguments that have given
direction to the field. They are grouped according
to the particular theory with which each article is
associated.

1. General:

Bengtson, Vern L.; and Haber, David A. "Sociological
Approaches to Aging." In Aging, edited by
Woodruff and Birren, pp. 70-91 (see annotation,
p. 48).

Busse, Ewald W. "Theories of Aging." In Behavior
and Adaptation in Late Life, edited by Busse
and Pfeiffer, pp. 11-32 (see citation, p. 66).

Maddox, George L. "Themes and Issues in Sociological Theories of Human Aging." Human Development 13 (1970): 17-27.

_____; and Wiley, James. "Scope, Concepts, and Methods in the Study of Aging." In Handbook of Aging and the Social Sciences, edited by Binstock and Shanas, pp. 3-34 (see annotation, p. 39).

2. Disengagement Theory:

Cumming, Elaine. "Further Thoughts on the Theory of Disengagement." International Social Science Journal 15 (1963): 377-393.

Havighurst, Robert B.; Neugarten, Bernice; and Tobin, Sheldon. "Disengagement and Patterns of Aging." In Middle Age and Aging, edited by Bernice Neugarten, pp. 161-172 (see annotation, p. 44).

Hochschild, Arlie R. "Disengagement Theory: A Critique and Proposal." American Sociological Review 40 (1975): 553-539.

Maddox, George L. "Disengagement Theory: A Critical Evaluation." The Gerontologist 4 (1964): 80-82.

Rose, Arnold M. "A Current Theoretical Issue in Social Gerontology." The Gerontologist 4 (1964): 46-50.

Youmans, E. Grant. "Some Perspectives on Disengagement Theory." The Gerontologist 9 (1969): 254-258.

3. Activity Theory:

Lemon, Bruce; Bengtson, Vern L.; and Peterson, James A. "An Exploration of the Activity Theory of Aging: Activity Types and Life Satisfaction Among In-Movers to a Retirement Community." Journal of Gerontology 27 (1972): 511-523.

4. Role Theory:

Cavan, Ruth. "Self and Role in Adjustment During Old Age." In Human Behavior and Social Processes, edited by Arnold Rose. Boston:

Houghton Mifflin, 1962, pp. 526-536.

Cottrell, L. S., Jr. "Adjustment of the Individual to His Age and Sex Roles." _American Sociological Review_ 7 (1942): 617-620.

Phillips, Bernard S. "A Role Theory Approach to Adjustment in Old Age." _American Sociological Review_ 22 (1957): 212-217.

5. Subculture of Aging:

Rose, Arnold M. "The Subculture of the Aging: A Framework for Research in Social Gerontology." In _Older People and Their Social World_, edited by Rose and Peterson, pp. 3-16 (see p. 45).

6. Other Theoretical Discussions:

Barron, Milton. "Minority Group Status of the Aged in American Society." _Journal of Gerontology_ 8 (1953): 477-482.

Dowd, James J. "Aging as Exchange: A Preface to Theory." _Journal of Gerontology_ 30 (1975): 584-594.

Kimmel, Douglas C. "Adulthood: Developmental Theory and Research." In _Adulthood and Aging: An Interdisciplinary, Developmental View_, by Douglas C. Kimmel, pp. 9-41 (see annotation, p. 44).

Kuypers, Joseph A.; and Bengtson, Vern L. "Social Breakdown and Competence: A Model of Normal Aging." _Human Development_ 16 (1973): 181-206.

Laslett, Peter. "Societal Development and Aging." In _Handbook of Aging and the Social Sciences_, edited by Binstock and Shanas, pp. 87-116 (see annotation, p. 39).

Neugarten, Bernice L. "Age Groups in American Society and the Rise of the Young-Old." _Annals of the American Association of Political and Social Sciences._ 415 (1974): 187-198.

_____; and Hagestad, Gunhild O. "Age and the Life Course." In _Handbook of Aging and the Social Sciences_, edited by Binstock and Shanas, pp. 35-55 (see annotation, p. 39).

Palmore, Erdman B.; and Manton, Kenneth. "Ageism Compared to Racism and Sexism." Journal of Gerontology 28 (1973): 363-369.

Riley, Matilda White. "Social Gerontology and the Age Stratification of Society." The Gerontologist 11 (1971): 79-87.

Ryder, Norman B. "The Cohort as a Concept in the Study of Social Change." American Sociological Review 30 (1965): 843-861.

Streib, Gordon F. "Are the Aged a Minority Group?" In Middle Age and Aging, edited by Neugarten, pp. 35-46 (see annotation, p. 44).

_____. "Social Stratification and Aging." In Handbook of Aging and the Social Sciences, edited by Binstock and Shanas, pp. 160-185 (see annotation, p. 39).

Youmans, E. Grant. "Age Stratification and Value Orientations." International Journal of Aging and Human Development 4 (1973): 53-65.

3
Physiological and Psychological Aspects of Aging

Much of the literature in this area is quite technical and difficult for even the informed lay reader to manage. Some of the most accessible presentations are those in anthologies and textbooks; often, however, these are oversimplified and frustrating to one who wants somewhat more detailed information. The list below is extremely general and does not reflect specializations within the field. There is, for example, a large body of literature on exercise and aging. The works listed here are representative of some of the better known writers on the physiology of aging. A number of them have written shorter pieces intended for the non-specialist, which, while still challenging, are helpful in providing an introduction to this aspect of aging.

PHYSIOLOGY AND BIOLOGY: ANNOTATED REFERENCES

BOOKS

Comfort, Alex. The Biology of Senescence. New York: Elsevier, 1978, 3rd edition.
 The best synthesis of the biology of aging that has been published. It includes all organisms including humans, and delves into theoretical discussions of topics such as mechanisms of aging, genetics of longevity and measurements of human aging rate. It is a technical and advanced text, by one of the leading writers in the field. It is not, however, inaccessible to the serious lay reader; the introductory and concluding essays are quite readable. The latter considers prolonging life in

comfortable and healthy ways. Extensive
bibliography.

Finch, Caleb; and Hayflick, Leonard, editors.
Handbook of the Biology of Aging. New York:
Van Nostrand Reinhold, 1977.
A comprehensive work of original articles;
part of the three-volume Handbook series. The book
is organized according to biological hierarchy,
beginning with the molecular level and moving up to
the organismic. As the introduction states, the
book "was designed for those readers, such as
graduate students and professionals in other areas
of science, who require a serious but fairly broad
discussion of specific biological aspects of aging."

Rockstein, Morris; and Sussman, Marvin. Biology of
Aging. Belmont, CA: Wadsworth Publishing Co.,
1979.
Probably the best general introduction to the
biology of human aging on the market. It covers
the process of aging on several levels - cellular
(theories of aging), organs and systems (the main
emphasis of the book), and populations (a small
amount of discussion here).

Rosenfeld, Albert. Prolongevity. New York: Avon,
1976.
A popular, somewhat flamboyant book suggesting
that longer life, without the negative aspects of
aging, is physiologically possible. Easy reading
and very useful for its presentation of well-known
writers and their theories. Extensive bibliography.

Saxon, Sue V.; and Etten, Mary Jean. Physical
Change and Aging: A Guide for the Helping
Professions. New York: Tiresias Press, 1978.
A short book, useful precisely because it is
intended for the beginning science reader. There is
a strong emphasis on the physical aspects of aging
with some discussion of social and psychological
dimensions. Discusses theories of aging, organ
systems, physical concerns such as drugs and
nutrition, and the possible behavioral consequences
of physiological aging. Good bibliography.

Shanas, Ethel. The Health of Older People: A
Social Survey. Cambridge: Harvard University,
1962.
Data for this study were collected in 1957 from
a nationwide sample of persons sixty-five and older

and from people to whom an older person would turn
in a health crisis. Although somewhat dated, this
remains a frequently cited report. The
questionnaires are included along with a section on
methodology.

Shock, Nathan, editor. Aging: Some Social and
    Biological Aspects. Washington, DC: American
    Association for the Advancement of Science,
    1960.
    These are papers from several symposia on aging
conducted in 1959. While there are some papers
on the social aspects of aging, most of the volume
is devoted to biological aging: tissues and cells,
cardiovascular changes, dental changes, etc. There
is a section devoted to theories of aging, physical
and otherwise. The articles range from elementary
to fairly sophisticated presentations.

Strehler, Bernard L. Time, Cells, and Aging. New
    York: Academic Press, 1977, 2nd edition.
    An important book, recently updated, that
documents the processes of biological aging with
special attention to cellular and sub-cellular
changes. The focus is on aging processes stemming
from genetic rather than environmental factors.
Like Comfort's monograph, this is an advanced work.
It is not overly technical, however. The author's
clear style, careful definitions and thorough
explanations make this a useful book for the serious
student. Good bibliography.

Tanner, J. M. Fetus Into Man. Cambridge, MA:
    Harvard University Press, 1978.
    An excellent summary of the process of growth
and development that includes discussion of how
different genetic and environmental factors affect
growth and maturation rates. It is written for the
non-biologist.

Timiras, P. S., editor. Developmental Physiology
    and Aging. New York: MacMillan Co., 1972.
    The second half of this frequently cited book
is devoted to the physiology of aging. The guiding
thesis of the work is that both genetic and environmental factors influence developmental and aging
processes; the body's adaptation mechanisms change
with age. The book presents both theoretical and
experimental research. Although it is a sophisticated presentation, it was intended for a broad
audience ranging from undergraduates to specialists

58

with either social science or biological backgrounds.
Full bibliographies along with in-depth special
selections for the interested reader.

Weg, Ruth B. Nutrition and the Later Years. Los
    Angeles: Ethel Percy Andrus Gerontology Center,
    University of Southern California, 1978.
    A basic book on the subject, designed primarily
for practitioners and service professionals. Some
useful summaries of physiological theories of aging.
Primarily concerned with nutritional requirements,
proper diet, pathologies and physiological behavior.
A glossary and extensive bibliography.

ARTICLES

Comfort, Alex. "Biological Theories of Aging."
    Human Development 13 (1970).
    Comfort is a highly respected biologist who
writes for both specialized and lay audiences. This
article briefly presents and critiques well known
theories of biological aging. It is a non-technical
piece intended for the lay reader.

Hayflick, Leonard. "Human Cells and Aging."
    Scientific American 218: 3 (1968): 32-37.
    An article addressed to the issues of longevity
and limited life-span. It concludes that "the
common impression that modern medicine has
lengthened the human life-span is not supported by
vital statistics or biological evidence." Like most
Scientific American pieces it is intended for the
interested non-specialist.

Rockstein, Morris. "The Biological Aspects of
    Aging." Gerontologist 8 (1968): 124-125.
    A short, concise summary of twelve major
physiological changes that occur with aging.

Goldstein, Samuel. "The Biology of Aging." New
    England Journal of Medicine 285 (1971): 1120-
    29.
    Definitely for the advanced reader with medical
or biological training. It is, however, intended
for the non-aging specialist and thus provides a
sophisticated introduction to the field.

Shock, Nathan W. "The Physiology of Aging."
    Scientific American 206 (1962): 100-110.
    A well-known article that provides a
straightforward explanation of physiological changes

and declines brought on by aging.

PHYSIOLOGY AND BIOLOGY: OTHER REFERENCES

Palmore, Erdman B.; and Jeffers, Frances C.,
     editors. Prediction of Life Span.
     Massachusetts: Heath Lexington Books, 1971.

Rockstein, Morris, editor. Theoretical Aspects of
     Aging. New York: Academic Press, 1974.

PSYCHOLOGY AND SOCIAL PSYCHOLOGY

     The psychology of aging is one of the most fully
explored areas of gerontology. Psychologists have
long been interested in the changes that may occur
as an individual grows older, and have sought to
account for these changes in a variety of ways.
There is a large body of literature focusing on
theoretical discussions as well as clinical and
experimental data. Research has examined several
dimensions of psychological processes: performance,
personality, and pathology. This research reflects
increasingly sophisticated methodologies,
particularly those intended to distinguish among
cohort, period, and age effects. A developmental
perspective--that the individual continues to grow
and change throughout life--has been widely adopted,
but not without challenge and controversy.

PSYCHOLOGY AND SOCIAL PSYCHOLOGY:
ANNOTATED REFERENCES
BOOKS

Aiken, Lewis. Later Life. Philadelphia: W. B.
     Saunders, 1978.
     Topics included are: biological factors,
mental abilities, personality development and
sexual behavior, mental disorders, employment and
retirement, health care, living environments and
activities, and death and bereavement. Although
the volume is multidisciplinary in content, its
author states that "the emphasis of the book is on
the psychology of later life." This is a basic
book--easy reading. Topics are summarized and
accompanied by suggestions for additional reading,
as well as a useful glossary of terms used in the
text.

Birren, James E. The Psychology of Aging. Englewood
    Cliffs, NY: Prentice-Hall, 1964.
    An early work by a prominent writer in the
field. It was designed as a textbook and is written
from a developmental perspective. Using research
findings available at the time, it has discussions
of: the social and cultural determinants of aging;
biological influences; sensory functioning and
perception; psychomotor activity; learning; thinking
and intelligence; employment, productivity and
achievement; personality; pathologies; and life
review. Each chapter is concluded with a helpful
and concise summary.

_____; and Schaie, K. Warner. Handbook of the
    Psychology of Aging. New York: Van Nostrand
    Reinhold, 1977.
    One of the three-volume series intended as
definitive review and reference works on social,
psychological and biological aspects of aging. The
series is designed for the use of graduate students,
researchers, and professionals in the field. Topics
covered in this volume include a broad range of
discussions of behavioral aspects of human aging,
age related changes in behavior and capacities, and
generational differences. Psychological phenomena
are related to social and biological influences.
There are comprehensive bibliographies throughout.

Botwinick, Jack. Aging and Behavior. New York:
    Springer, 1973.
    A useful text, designed for undergraduates,
although some technical material will be more useful
to teachers and researchers. Discussions focus on
both the performance and personality dimensions of
psychological aging. The author reviews many
important studies, and discusses various theories
of aging. There is a very good concluding chapter
on research methodology which discusses cross-
sectional, longitudinal and time-lag research
designs.

_____. Cognitive Processes in Maturity and Old
    Age. New York: Springer, 1967.
    A somewhat more advanced work than above.
Again, the author refers to a number of experimental
studies and considers theoretical questions as well.
He is concerned with understanding the problems
and concerns of old age as they relate to total
life span development. There are chapters on
intelligence; learning; memory and forgetting;

thinking, problem solving and creativity.

Britton, Joseph H.; and Britton, Jean O. Personality Changes in Aging: A Longitudinal Study of Community Residents. New York: Springer, 1972. Although the data upon which this book is based were collected in the 1950's, it remains a useful study in terms of methodology and substance. Subjects who were initially aged 65 and over were tested on three occasions over a nine year period. The authors wanted to determine how consistent personality patterns are over time, and to identify the social and psychological correlates of survival to old age. Unlike most aging studies, the sample was drawn from a rural community. The study and analysis are carefully described; the full interview schedule is included.

Bromley, Dennis B. The Psychology of Human Ageing. Baltimore: Penguin Books, 1966. A well-known book by an English author that is addressed to a general non-technical audience. It is rather dated in theoretical perspective. Biological and social phenomena are related to psychological aspects of aging. There are discussions of behavior, mental skills and personality, as well as psychopathology and mental disease.

Butler, Robert N.; and Lewis, Myrna I. Aging and Mental Health--Positive Psychosocial Approaches. St. Louis: C. V. Mosby, 1977, 2nd edition. Although intended for social workers and others who serve the elderly, this book should be useful to a more general audience. It is a clearly written and well documented presentation of emotional and psychological problems which confront the elderly. The second half of the book is devoted to evaluation, treatment and prevention. The emphasis throughout is a positive one; the authors stress ways in which the elderly can contribute to their own care and improved psychological functioning. There are excellent appendices which include sources of literature, and other educational material, names of organizations pertaining to the elderly, government programs, grant programs and social services, training programs, and a glossary.

Eisdorfer, Carl; and Lawton, M. Powell, editors. The Psychology of Adult Development and Aging. Washington, DC: American Psychological Association,

1973.

A collection of essays for the advanced student. The articles cover most of the psychological specialities, ranging from pieces based on animal research to discussions of psychophysiology, and transportation and housing. Experimental, developmental and clinical approaches are all represented. This book is a report on the state of the profession at the time and concludes with a position paper intended for the 1971 White House conference on aging. There are some excellent bibliographies which include review and state-of-the-art articles.

Howells, John G., editor. Modern Perspectives in the Psychiatry of Old Age. New York: Brunner/ Mazel, 1975.

An advanced text intended for the practicing clinician. There are, however, a number of essays (e.g. "Sexual Behavior," "Facing Death") which should be useful to the serious student. The collection represents a comprehensive, international approach to a wide range of psychiatric issues relevant to aging. Some of the topics included are: genetics, psychopathology, depression and suicide, historical perspectives on care, hospital and community care, and expressions of psychopathology in art. A number of prominent writers in the field are represented.

Kalish, Richard A. Late Adulthood: Perspectives on Human Development. Monterey, CA: Brooks/Cole, 1975.

A basic text that is easy to read and is quite general in content. The author's purpose is to provide a psychological perspective. He discusses the "imperatives" (physical and psychological) of aging as well as personality, human relationships, and environments.

Kastenbaum, Robert, editor. New Thoughts on Old Age. New York: Springer, 1964.

A collection of twenty-five essays by social scientists and clinicians; all but five are original. There are five sections: theoretical perspectives; psychological and social correlates of longevity; clinical experiences with the aged (e.g. institutionalization, therapy); attitudes toward aging by young and old; and the organization of experience in later life. The last is especially interesting and covers a relatively unexplored area of the aging process.

Lowenthal, Marjorie Fiske; and Berkman, Paul L; and
Associates. Aging and Mental Disorder in San
Francisco: A Social Psychiatric Study. San
Francisco: Jossey-Bass, 1967.
One of a series of studies on aging produced
by researchers associated with the Langley Porter
Neuropsychiatric Institute in San Francisco. The
focus of many of these studies is the causes and
conditions of mental health and illness among the
aged. The data were collected in the early 1960's
from two samples--one a group of psychiatrically
hospitalized elderly, the other a random sample of
elderly in the community. This volume focuses
primarily on the community sample. It identifies
sociocultural and physical correlates of mental
illness; compares the community subjects to the
hospitalized sample; and describes, but does not
usually account for, change over time in mental
health status. The authors consider the issue of
change in intellectual functioning in the elderly.
There are discussions of methodological and
theoretical issues throughout. The baseline
questionnaire for the community sample is included.

_____; Thurnher, Majda; Chiriboga, David; and
Associates. Four Stages of Life: A Comparative
Study of Women and Men Facing Transitions. San
Francisco: Jossey-Bass, 1975.
Later life is only one of the four stages
described in this "sociopsychological field study."
High school seniors, young newlyweds, and middle-
aged parents also constitute groups facing
transitions. The fourth group is older people about
to retire. The general theme of the book is
adaptation to change. The subjects are drawn from
the middle and lower middle-class. There are
several chapters devoted to discussions of
methodology and measures.

Neugarten, Bernice L., et al. Personality in Middle
and Late Life: Empirical Studies. New York:
Atherton Press, 1964.
A collection of studies of personality based
on data gathered for the Kansas City Studies of
Adult Life. Both social and psychological factors
of middle age and aging were considered. Topics
include: personality and adjustment; age and sex
roles; ego functions; personality types; and
personality and social interaction. This volume
represents an early effort in developmental
psychology, and as such is important historically

64

as well as substantively. There are eight studies
representing a variety of theoretical and
methodological approaches and a methodological
chapter is included. Neugarten provides a helpful
introduction and summary. The writing is clear;
some knowledge of basic psychology is useful.

Pitt, Bruce. Psychogeriatrics: An Introduction to
the Psychiatry of Old Age. Edinborough and
London: Churchill Livingstone, 1974.
An English work that is decidedly national in
terms of statistics and examples. However, it is
intended for a general audience and has some clear
explanations of various psychiatric pathologies
among the aged. It will probably be most useful to
service workers and practitioners.

Rosenfeld, Anne H. New Views on Older Lives: A
Sampler of NIMH Sponsored Research and Service
Programs. Rockville, MD: National Institute
of Mental Health, U.S. Department of Health,
Education and Welfare, 1978.
A short report summarizing recent NIMH-sponsored
research. The studies included here examined such
topics as lifestyle and life satisfaction; community
services; institutionalization; depression and
senility. The book is clearly written and provides
a good introduction to ongoing research in the
field.

Zinberg, Norman E.; and Kaufman, Irving, editors.
Normal Psychology of the Aging Process. New
York: International Universities Press, 1978.
2nd edition.
This collection of papers by professionals is
intended for other professionals. A reader with a
grounding in psychology should find the book useful.
In general, the authors acknowledge developmental
and psychoanalytic perspectives. They present
discussions of: cultural and personality factors
associated with aging; psychosocial and
sociophysiological approaches to aging; intrapsychic
aspects of aging; regression and recession in the
psychoses of aging; social learning and self-image;
marital adaptation; and sexuality and aging.

ARTICLES

Baltes, Paul; and Schaie, K. Warner. "Aging and IQ:
The Myth of the Twilight Years." Psychology
Today. 7 (March, 1974): 35-40.

A popular, clearly stated presentation of one side of the aging and IQ controversy. These authors have argued throughout their writings that intelligence does not inevitably decline with age. Those test results that seem to demonstrate such a decline are, they argue, actually due to cohort phenomena. The authors dispute their leading critic, John Horne, whose writings should also be read to provide a balanced view. Baltes and Schaie subscribe to a developmental approach.

Butler, Robert N. "The Life Review: An Interpretation of Reminiscence in the Aged." Psychiatry 26 (1963): 65-76.
A well known, frequently reprinted article that theorizes on the nature and purpose of reminiscence by the aged. The life review, argues Butler, actually goes beyond reminiscence, which is just one component in a psychological preparation for death. This is a stimulating discussion of an often reported, but little understood phenomenon.

Edwards, K. A. "Restoring Functional Behavior of 'Senile' Elderly." In J. M. Ferguson and C. B. Taylor, editors. The Comprehensive Handbook of Behavioral Medicine: Extended Applications and Issues. Vol. 3. Jamaica, NY: SP Medical and Scientific Books, in press.
Reviews the history, theory, and applications of "senility" and describes some possible strategies for restoring functional behavior in this population of the elderly.

Havighurst, Robert J. "A Social-psychological Perspective on Aging." The Gerontologist 8 (1968): 67-71.
A short article that is useful for its history of the Kansas City studies and the books that resulted from that research.

Poggi, Raymond G.; and Berland, David. "Newcomer's Group: A Preliminary Report." Journal of the National Association of Private Psychiatric Hospitals 10: 1 (1978): 47-51.
This article is written from the perspective of two therapists who led an expressive psychotherapy group in a retirement home. It is a clearly written account of the problems of making the transition from independent community living to residence in a retirement home. The authors identify several stages of psychological adjustment that precede

moving to the home.

Schaie, K. Warner; and Gribbin, Kathy. "Adult
    Development and Aging." Annual Review of
    Psychology. 26 (1975): 65-96.
    A literature review covering the years 1968 to
1973. The emphasis is on a developmental
perspective. The authors consider methodological
issues, books on adult development, and major
contributions to the research literature.

PSYCHOLOGY AND SOCIAL PSYCHOLOGY:
OTHER REFERENCES

BOOKS

Barrett, J. H. Gerontological Psychology.
    Springfield, IL: Charles C. Thomas, 1972.

Bengtson, Vern L. The Social Psychology of Aging.
    Indianapolis: Bobbs-Merrill, 1973.

Busse, Ewald W.; and Pfeiffer, Eric, editors.
    Behavior and Adaptation in Late Life. Boston:
    Little, Brown and Co., 1969.

_____, editors. Mental Illness in Later
    Life. Washington, DC: American Psychiatric
    Association, 1973.

Kalish, Richard A., editor. The Dependencies of Old
    People. Ann Arbor: Institute of Gerontology,
    The University of Michigan--Wayne State
    University, 1969.

Levin, Sidney; and Kahana, Ralph J., editors.
    Psychodynamic Studies on Aging: Creativity,
    Reminiscing, and Dying. Boston Society for
    Gerontologic Psychiatry. New York:
    International Universities Press, 1967.

ARTICLES

Butler, Robert N. "Psychiatry and the Elderly: An
    Overview." American Journal of Psychiatry
    132 (1975): 893-900.

Havighurst, Robert J. "Personalities and Patterns of Aging." The Gerontologist 8 (1968):20-23.

AN ADDENDUM ON METHODOLOGY

A thorough treatment of the methodological literature on human development and aging would be more appropriate in a bibliography intended for advanced students and scholars. We include, here, two works that are likely to prove particularly helpful to beginning students.

Baltes, Paul B.; Reese, Hayne W.; and Nesselroade, John R. Life-Span Developmental Psychology: Introduction to Research Methods. Monterey, CA: Brooks/Cole, 1977.

As the title suggests, there is an emphasis on research design and methodology. Although the book does not focus specifically on the elderly, it is an excellent introduction to theories and procedures now being employed in research on aging. It provides clear explanations of many concepts associated with research methodology (e.g., validity and reliability, models, testing effects, and cohort analysis), and provides illustrations and examples throughout. It includes an extensive bibliography.

Glenn, Norval D. Cohort Analysis. Beverly Hills, CA: Sage, 1977.

Cohort designs are especially important in the study of aging processes. While the examples provided here are predominantly taken from political research, this 72-page monograph is an exceptionally lucid introduction to the fundamental concepts and problems of cohort analysis.

4
Social Aspects of Aging

Old people, like all human beings, are part of
a larger world which influences their lives.
Policies, services, and programs created by
government are one dimension of that world. In
addition, most people move through life as members
of various groups (e.g., political, occupational,
economic, ethnic, and religious) and membership in
such groups can affect the aging process. Thus, a
number of works examine the relationships that exist
between the old person and various social
institutions. Much of the analysis of this type
considers older people as a total population--an
aggregate--although there is increasing insistence
by many that individual and subgroup differences
must be recognized.

DEATH AND DYING

There has been an enormous outpouring of
literature in this field in recent years. It is
often an emotionally charged issue which raises
profound legal, moral, ethical, religious, medical,
psychological, and economic questions. While much
of the writing does not focus specifically on the
aged, the implicit assumption in many works is that
most people will be old when they die. Many of the
books and articles in this area are intended as aids
for those who work with the dying, and for the
family and friends who must cope with dying and the
grief that follows.

DEATH AND DYING: ANNOTATED REFERENCES

BOOKS

Ariĕs, Phillippe. Western Attitudes Toward Death
from the Middle Ages to the Present.
Translated by Patricia M. Ranum. Baltimore:
Johns Hopkins University Press, 1974.
Four essays tracing attitudes toward death from
the open, highly ritualized practices of medieval
times to the fearful and often secretive tendencies
of modern times. These are thoughtful, well written
pieces that offer a humane perspective on the subject.

Fulton, Robert, editor. Death and Identity. New
York: John Wiley and Sons, 1965.
A collection of essays that includes both
theoretical and empirical studies. At least seven
of the articles focus specifically on the aged,
discussing attitudes and responses toward death and
the grieving process. There is an extensive
bibliography.

Jury, Mark; and Jury, Dan. Gramp. New York:
Grossman Publishers, A Division of the Viking
Press, 1976.
Presents a moving, pictorial essay of the
death of a grandfather. It chronicles the struggle
of an eighty-one year old man's desire to have a
"good" death and the struggle of a family to assist
an elder member to die at home with his dignity
intact. The real and human interrelationships of a
family faced with the death of a beloved grandparent
are documented over a three-year span of time.

Kalish, Richard A.; and Reynolds, David K. Death
and Ethnicity: A Psychocultural Study. Los
Angeles: Ethel Percy Andrus Gerontology
Center, University of Southern California,
1976.
A cross-cultural study of attitudes towards
death, treatment of the dying, and funeral customs
among American ethnic groups. The groups surveyed
included Black, Japanese, Mexican and Anglo-
Americans. The authors considered a number of
variables in their study, including age, sex,
education and reliogisity. The book includes their
complete statistical analysis as well as an
extensive bibliography.

Kastenbaum, Robert and Aisenberg, Ruth. The
Psychology of Death. New York: Springer
Publishing Company, 1972. Paperback edition
(shortened version), 1976.
A useful, well-referenced resource which
emphasizes the theoretical contributions made by
social and behavioral scientists. The scope is
broad, and focuses upon man's relationship to and
attitudes about death; psychological factors in
dying and longevity, suicide and murder; and the
cultural milieu in which death occurs in today's
society. The latter includes a discussion about
professionals who encounter the death system most
frequently, i.e., the physician, nurse, mental health
professional, funeral director, and clergyman.

Kubler-Ross, Elisabeth. On Death and Dying. New
York: The Macmillan Company, 1969.
This work is introduced by a discussion of
societal attitudes and influences which have
fostered the death denial phenomena in the United
States. Kubler-Ross' work with more than 200 dying
patients resulted in identification of five
observable stages in the dying process: anger,
denial, bargaining, depression, and acceptance.
Each stage is defined, described and illustrated by
case reports and interviews with dying patients.
The shared agony and expectations of the dying
provide greater insight into the final stage of life
with all its anxieties, fears and hopes. A classic
in the field.

Pattinson, E. Mansell. The Experience of Dying.
Englewood Cliffs, NJ: Prentice-Hall, Inc.,
1977.
Psychiatrist E. Mansell Pattison's framework
for understanding the dying process is divided into
three phases: 1) the acute phase, 2) the chronic
living-dying phase, and 3) the terminal phase.
Attendant emotional reactions in each phase are
explicated. A major portion of the book provides
individual portraits of the dying process in all
stages of the life cycle, i.e., early and middle
childhood, adolescence, young adulthood, middle and
old age. A helpful, topical bibliography is
included for further study.

Weisman, Avery D. On Dying and Denying: A
Psychiatric Study of Terminality. New York:
Behavioral Publications, 1972.
The emphasis in this book is on the experience

of those dying from terminal illness. There is one
chapter devoted to the terminally ill aged. The
author, a clinical psychiatrist, uses case studies
to develop a theoretical discussion of death and
dying. This is an elementary, readable book.

ARTICLES

Gustafson, Elizabeth. "Dying: The Career of the
     Nursing Home Patient." Journal of Health and
     Social Behavior 13 (1972): 226-35.
An application of Roth's "career timetable"
format to the experiences of old people in nursing
homes. The author suggests that both staff and
patients follow a certain pattern of behavior that
can be categorized into several stages. The
expectation of death shapes this behavior.

Marshall, Victor W. "Socialization for Impending
     Death in a Retirement Village." American
     Journal of Sociology. LXXX (1975): 1124-44.
The conclusions in this article are based on
fieldwork conducted by the author in 1969-70 in a
Canadian retirement village. The author suggests
that preparation for death is the final "role
adjustment," and that successful adjustment can be
facilitated by congregate residences such as a
retirement village. The residents are viewed as
active participants in their "collective
socialization for impending death."

DEATH AND DYING: OTHER REFERENCES

Parkes, Colin Murray. Bereavement, Studies of Grief
     in Adult Life. New York: International
     Universities Press, 1972.

Shibles, Warren. Death: An Interdisciplinary
     Analysis. Whitewater, WI: Language Press,
     1974.

Sudnow, David. Passing On: The Social Organization
     of Dying. Englewood Cliffs, NJ: Prentice-Hall,
     1967.

Van Tassel, David, editor. Aging, Death and the
     Completion of Being. Philadelphia: University
     of Pennsylvania, 1979.

Vernon, Glenn. Sociology of Death: An Analysis of
     Death Related Behavior. New York: Ronald

Press, 1970.

DEMOGRAPHY

Demography is the study of populations--their size, patterns of growth and decline, and composition. Demographers study patterns of change within the population as measured by age, sex, marriage and divorce, income, occupation, migration, and so forth. Demographic studies are, of course, essential to understanding the dramatically increased numbers of elderly within our population, their present behavior, and future trends.

DEMOGRAPHY: ANNOTATED REFERENCES

BOOKS

National Council on the Aging. Fact Book on Aging: A Profile of America's Older Population. Washington, DC: The National Council on the Aging, 1976.
A compendium of statistical data on the elderly, drawn from a wide variety of sources. Most of the data is from 1975. This is a summary volume, designed for ready reference, not comprehensive research.

ARTICLES

Some of the most useful discussions are chapters on demography and aging included in a number of textbooks and anthologies. Among the more helpful are:

Coale, Ansley J. "How A Population Ages or Grows Younger." In Population: The Vital Revolution, edited by Ronald Freedman. Garden City, NY: Anchor Books, 1964.

Cutler, Neal E. and Robert A. Harootyan. "Demography of the Aged." In Aging: Scientific Perspectives and Social Issues, edited by Diana S. Woodruff and James E. Birren. New York: Van Nostrand, 1975.

Hauser, Philip M. "Aging and World-Wide Population Change." In Handbook of Aging and the Social Sciences, edited by Robert H. Binstock and Ethel Shanas. New York: Van Nostrand Reinhold, 1976.

GOVERNMENT PUBLICATIONS

Some of the most valuable information about
old people in this country--the same data that
demographers use--is supplied by the U.S.
government in the form of census reports and
population analyses. Current Population Reports, a
series published by the U.S. Census Bureau, has a
number of issues on older Americans. Some
representative titles are listed below along with
some other government documents, all of whose titles
are self-explanatory

Bixby, Lenore J.; Finegar, Wayne W.; Grod, Susan;
    Kolodrubetz, Walter W.; Lauriat, Patience; and
    Murray, Janet H. Demographic and Economic
    Characteristics of the Aged: 1968 Social
    Security Survey. Research Report No. 45.
    Office of Research and Statistics. Washington,
    DC: U.S. Government Printing Office, 1975.

Bouvier, Leon F.; Atlee, Elinore; and McVeigh,
    Frank. "The Elderly in America." In
    Population Bulletin, v. 30, no. 3. Washington,
    DC: Population Reference Bureau, 1976.

Epstein, Lenore Alice; and Murray, Janet H. The
    Aged Population of the United States: The 1963
    Social Security Survey of the Aged. Research
    Report No. 19. U.S. Social Security
    Administration, Office of Research and
    Statistics, Washington, DC: U.S. Government
    Printing Office, 1967.

Irelan, Lola M.; Motley, Dena K., Schwab, Karen;
    Sherman, Sally R.; and Murray, Janet. Almost
    65: Baseline Data from the Retirement History
    Study. Research Report No. 49. U.S. Social
    Security Administration, Office of Research and
    Statistics. Washington, DC: U.S. Government
    Printing Office, 1976.

Siegel, Jacob S. "Demographic Aspects of Aging and
    the Older Population in the United States."
    Current Population Reports, Special Studies
    Series P-23, no. 59. U.S. Bureau of the Census.
    Washington, DC: U.S. Government Printing
    Office, 1976.
Appendix B of this Report is a "List of Sources
or Guides to Sources of Census Bureau Data on the
Older Population."

Statistical Reports on Older Americans. Issued
     periodically since 1976 by the National
     Clearinghouse on Aging, U.S. Administration on
     Aging, Washington, DC. This publication
     replaced an earlier series edited by Herman
     Brotman entitled Facts and Figures on Older
     Americans. Washington, DC: Department of
     Health, Education and Welfare, Administration
     on Aging, 1971-75.
     Brotman has written several demographic
analyses of older Americans and is a useful name to
watch for in anthologies and journals.

U.S. Bureau of the Census. "Population Estimates
     and Projections, Projections of the Population
     of the United States, by Age and Sex: 1977-
     2060." Current Population Reports. Series
     P-25, no. 704. Washington, DC: U.S.
     Government Printing Office, 1977.

_____. "Some Demographic Aspects of Aging in the
     United States." Current Population Reports.
     Series P-23, no. 43. Washington, DC: U.S.
     Government Printing Office, 1973.

_____. "Social and Economic Characteristics of
     the Older Population." Current Population
     Report. Series P-23, no. 57. Washington, DC:
     U.S. Government Printing Office, 1975.

U.S. Department of Health, Education and Welfare.
     The Elderly Population: Estimates by County,
     1976. DHEW Pub. No. (OHDS) 78-20248.
     Washington, DC: National Clearinghouse on
     Aging, U.S. Administration on Aging, 1978.

ECONOMICS AND RETIREMENT

     The economic status of the elderly is affected
by a variety of factors including personal planning
and resources, employment history, and the state
of the economy generally. Most, but not all, people
over age 65 do not work. Most, but not all, count
on some outside sources of income ranging from a
retirement pension to social security and old age
assistance programs sponsored by the government.
The literature in the field focuses on economic
status of the aged, various government and private
retirement programs, and the economic impact of an
ever-increasing number of aged on the rest of the
economy. In addition, there is a large body of

76

literature on retirement per se--its social as well
as economic characteristics.

ECONOMICS: ANNOTATED REFERENCES

BOOKS

Brittain, John A. The Payroll Tax for Social
    Security. Washington, DC: The Brookings
    Institution, 1972.
    An examination of the methods and inequities
of the regressive FICA tax, a component of the
social security financing system.

Derthick, Martha. Policymaking for Social Security.
    Washington, DC: The Brookings Institution,
    1979.
    A presentation of the development and current
problems and politics of the Social Security system
(OASDHI). The book suggests the possible nature and
condition of Social Security financing in the
future.

Herzog, Barbara R. Aging and Income. New York:
    Human Sciences Press, 1978.
    A consideration of the impact of increasing
numbers of elderly on income and retirement.

Orbach, Harold; and Tibbitts, Clark, editors. Aging
    and the Economy. Ann Arbor, MI: University
    of Michigan Press, 1963.
    A collection of papers from a 1962 conference.
The topics covered include: the relation of the
national economy to the older population; employment
opportunities; income and other resources; consumer
potential; pension funds; and the development of
public policy.

Rosenberg, George S. The Worker Grows Old: Poverty
    and Isolation in the City. San Francisco:
    Jossey-Bass, 1970.
    A book that deals with the social isolation of
the working class. It is an effort to reconcile
theories concerning the isolation of the elderly
with those which account for working class
isolation. As such, the book is actually much
broader than an "economic" study. The conclusions
are drawn from a survey of white working class
Philadelphians between the ages of forty-five and
seventy-nine.

Rosenfeld, Jeffrey P. Legacy of Aging: Inheritance
     and Disinheritance in Social Perspective.
     Norwood, NJ: Ablex Publishing Corp., 1979.
     An examination of the patterns of inheritance
with special focus on the social characteristics of
will writers. The author examines relationships
between certain lifestyles and patterns of
inheritance, and considers the question of
inheritance as a linking mechanism within families.

Schulz, James H. The Economics of Aging. 2nd ed.
     Belmont, CA: Wadsworth, 1980.
     Perhaps the standard work on the subject. It
is very readable; includes glossary of specialized
terms. The author discusses and explains the
economic relationship of the older population to the
rest of the country; retirement, pensions and social
security; trends in work-force participation by
older workers, income adequacy and management; and
issues for future concern. Excellent bibliographies.

                        ARTICLES

     In addition to the regular gerontological
publications, there are two periodical sources that
are especially helpful in this area:
     Industrial Gerontology, a quarterly published
by the National Council on the Aging; and the
     Social Security Bulletin, published monthly
since 1938 by the U.S. Social Security
Administration.

Havighurst, Robert J. "The Future Aged: The Use of
     Time and Money." The Gerontologist 15 (1975):
     10-14.
     A speculative discussion of the impact of
changing demography and economics on retirement and
the elderly.

              ECONOMICS: OTHER REFERENCES

Barsby, Steve L.; and Cox, Dennis R. Interstate
     Migration of the Elderly: An Economic Analysis.
     Lexington, MA: Lexington Books, 1975.

Brennan, Michael J.; Taft, Philip; and Schupack,
     Mark B. The Economics of Age. New York: W. W.
     Norton and Co., 1967.

Claque, Ewan; Pall, Palraj; Kramer, Leo. The Aging
     Worker and the Union: Employment and Retirement

of Middle Aged and Older Workers. New York:
Praeger Publishers, 1971.

Hoskins, Dalmer; and Bixby, Lenore E. Women and
Social Security: Law and Policy in Five
Countries. U.S. Department of Health,
Education and Welfare, Social Security
Administration. Research Report no. 42.
Washington, DC: U.S. Government Printing
Office, 1973.

Kreps, Juanita M., et. al. The Economic Implications
For Older Americans of a Stable Population.
Durham, NC: Duke Center for the Study of Aging
and Human Development, 1976.

_____, editor. Employment, Income, and
Retirement Problems of the Aged. Durham, NC:
Duke University Press, 1963.

_____. Lifetime Allocation of Work and Income:
Essays in the Economics of Aging. Durham, NC:
Duke University Press, 1971.

Osterbind, Carter C., editor. New Careers for Older
People. Gainesville: University of Florida
Press, 1971.

Rosenberg, George S. Poverty, Aging and Social
Isolation. Washington, DC: Bureau of Social
Science Research, 1967.

Sheppard, Harold L. Industrial Gerontology.
Cambridge, MA: Schenkman, 1970.

_____. New Perspectives on Older Workers.
Kalamazoo, MI: W. E. Upjohn Institute for
Employment Research, 1971.

_____; and Rix, Sara E. The Graying of Working
America: The Coming Crisis in Retirement Age
Policy. New York: The Free Press, 1977.

RETIREMENT: ANNOTATED REFERENCES

BOOKS

Atchley, Robert C. The Sociology of Retirement.
Cambridge: Schenkman; and New York: Halsted
Press/John Wiley and Sons, 1976.
A good introduction to the subject which

provides an historical perspective as well as an analysis of the social, psychological, and economic aspects of retirement. It offers critiques of past theories and suggests a new theoretical perspective as a means for understanding the retirement process. As with other Atchley writings, an excellent bibliography is included

Carp, Frances M., editor. <u>Retirement</u>. New York: Behavioral Publications, 1972.
  Papers produced for a 1966 conference on retirement. This is a useful interdisciplinary book with articles by a number of well-known scholars in the field who discuss retirement from psychological, sociological, anthropological, medical and economic perspectives. The anthropological piece (Margaret Clark) in particular provides a background not usually presented.

Ingraham, Mark H. <u>My Purpose Holds: Reactions and Experiences in Retirement of TIAA-CREF Annuitants</u>. New York: TIAA-CREF, 1974.
  The Teachers Insurance and Annuity Association of America and College Retirement Equities Fund represent one of the largest insurance and retirement pension packages in the country. The retired annuitants, the majority of whom were associated with academic institutions, were surveyed in 1972. This is a report of the responses to open-ended questions on problems, personal evaluations and experiences and advice to future retirees. Little analysis; for the most part a compilation of quotations appropriate to the designated categories.

Streib, Gordon F.; and Schneider, Clement J. <u>Retirement in American Society: Impact and Process</u>. Ithaca, NY: Cornell University Press, 1971.
  Report of a national, longitudinal study (1952-1958) of older workers, begun while they were still employed and continued through the first six years of retirement. Authors compared pre-retirement expectations to actual experience and found that the majority surveyed considered retirement better than they had expected.

RETIREMENT: OTHER REFERENCES

BOOKS

Barfield, Richard E.; and Morgan, James N.   Early
    Retirement: The Decision and the Experience
    and The Automobile Worker and Retirement: A
    Second Look.   Ann Arbor, MI: Institute for
    Social Research, University of Michigan, 1974.

Carp, Frances M.   The Retirement Process.
    Washington, DC: U.S. Government Printing
    Office, 1968.

Friedman, Eugene A.; Havighurst, Robert J.; and
    Harlan, William H., editors.   The Meaning of
    Work and Retirement.   Chicago: University of
    Chicago Press, 1954.

Havighurst, Robert J.; Munnichs, Joep M. A.;
    Neugarten, Bernice L.; and Thomae, Hans,
    editors.   Adjustment to Retirement: A Cross-
    National Study.   Assen, The Netherlands: Van
    Gorcum, 1972, 3rd unrev. ed.

ARTICLES

Kimmel, Douglas C.; Price, Karl F.; and Walker,
    James W.   "Retirement Choice and Retirement
    Satisfaction."   Journal of Gerontology 33
    (1978):   575-585.

Palmore, Erdman.   "Why Do People Retire?"   Aging and
    Human Development 2 (1971):   269-283.

ETHNICITY

Another dimension of the social world of the
elderly is ethnic identity which may have its
origins in racial, national, or religious roots.
Ethnic affiliation can influence the formation of
friendships, relations with kin, foodways and
celebration of festivals and holidays, as well as
attitudes toward pain and death, standards of success
and achievement, and expectations of growing old.
Gerontologists have been aware of ethnic differences
between black and white elderly.   The discussion has
expanded to include Orientals and Native Americans
and, finally, white ethnics.   Some writings stress
the "minority" status of ethnic aged, pointing out
the extremely disadvantaged situation of these

people, while others emphasize the cultural features of the various ethnic groups that shape the lives of older people. Because of the relatively recent attention given to the issue of ethnicity and aging, much useful information is still in periodical form.

ETHNICITY: ANNOTATED REFERENCES

BOOKS

Clark, Margaret; and Anderson, Barbara. Culture and Aging: An Anthropological Study of Older Americans. Springfield, IL: Charles C. Thomas, 1967.
A now standard account of a study of elderly people in San Francisco, a group which included members of ethnic communities. The authors measured morale and self-esteem among a group of older people representing varying degrees of mental health. They concluded that differences among their subjects were due to a number of factors including ethnicity.

Coles, Robert. The Old Ones of New Mexico. Albuquerque, NM: University of New Mexico Press, 1973.
A short, sensitive account of attitudes held by and about older people who still live in a largely traditional rural setting in the New Mexican mountains. Presented in sharply drawn vignettes and anecdotes.

Cowgill, Donald; and Holmes, Lowell D., editors. Aging and Modernization. New York: Appleton-Century-Crofts, 1972.
An early collection of essays, a number of which first appeared in The Gerontologist, representing a cross-cultural analysis of the aging process. Groups considered range from tribal organizations to advanced western societies. The authors applied a modernization model to the different groups and concluded that modernization has a negative impact on the elderly.

Gelfand, Donald E.; and Kutzik, Alfred J., editors. Ethnicity and Aging: Theory, Research, and Policy. New York: Springer, 1979.
The first comprehensive volume in the field. It represents a state-of-the-art assessment and includes discussions of theory, policy development, and ethnic families; and findings from research in a

number of areas including support networks,
emotional and psychological needs and changes,
service delivery, and institutionalization.

Jackson, Jacquelyne. Minorities and Aging. Belmont,
    CA: Wadsworth Publishing, 1980.
    A discussion of aging, with ample illustrations
of aging among minorities. It contains demographic
aspects of minority aging, physiological aspects of
aging, mortality and life expectancy patterns of
aging minorities, psychological aspects of minority
aging, social problems of the aged minorities and
Federal policies. The last chapter considers some
important issues about the future of minority
elderly.
    This new work presents an excellent up-date
of earlier literature reviews, thus providing
interested readers in this field with a basic
research tool as well as reference materials.

Kalish, Richard; and Reynolds, David K. Death and
    Ethnicity: A Psychocultural Study. Los
    Angeles: Ethel Percy Andrus Gerontology Center,
    University of Southern California, 1976. (see
    annotation, p. 70).

Kiefer, Christie. Changing Cultures, Changing
    Lives. San Francisco: Jossey-Bass, 1974.
    Analysis of inter-generational cultural
conflict among three generations of Japanese
Americans. Kiefer has written some articles as
well, documenting the impact of racial
discrimination and the upheaval of World War II on
traditional Japanese patterns of filial duty.

Myerhoff, Barbara; and Simić, Andrei, editors.
    Life's Career--Aging: Cultural Variations on
    Growing Old. Beverly Hills: Sage, 1978.
    An anthropological approach to aging which
emphasizes understanding the old person in the total
context of family and social life. This book
includes five studies: the Chagga of Mt. Kilimanjaro;
the elderly in Yugoslavia and Mexico; and Jewish-
American and Mexican-American aged. The studies
are linked by the editors' theoretical introduction
and conclusion, and by a common methodology.

Proceedings of the Research Conference on Minority
    Group Aged in the South, October, 1971.
    Durham, ND: Center for the Study on Aging and
    Human Development, Duke University Medical

Center, April, 1972.
A collection of papers, the majority of which
focus on the experience of the black elderly.

Sherman, George, editor. Research and Training in
     Minority Aging. Washington, DC: National
     Center on the Black Aged, 1978.
A volume that presents a number of concerns
and suggestions for research and training for
minority aging. There is an emphasis on the
undeveloped state of the art, the poverty of current
research methodologies and activities, and the lack
of training resources, especially for minorities.
The author strongly suggests that program developers
should lay the foundations for developing minority
components in gerontological programs.

Simmons, Leo. The Role of the Aged in Primitive
     Society. New Haven, CT: Yale, 1945.
Although dated and methodologically flawed,
this remains a classic anthropological survey of the
aged in pre-industrial societies. It considers
attitudes toward and treatment of the elderly in a
variety of settings ranging from primitive tribes of
gatherers to fairly settled agricultural groups.
Simmons' work has been used by some who argue that
modernization has a negative impact on the lives of
the elderly.

U.S. Congress, Senate Special Committee on Aging.
     Multiple Hazards of Age and Race, The
     Situation of Aged Blacks in the U.S.
     Washington, DC: U.S. Government Printing
     Office, 1971.
A comparison of the status of black and white
senior citizens, problems of lifestyles, population
and distribution, income, employment, unemployment,
social and emotional problems, relating to
industrialization, urbanization and automation, and
who to solve these problems. Racial composition of
Social Security beneficiaries and the objectives,
goals and purpose of the National Caucus on the
Black Aged are also covered.

U.S. Department of Commerce. Social and Economic
     Status of the Black Population in the United
     States. Washington, DC, 1973.
A report on the black population with
statistics, graphs, tables, employment,
unemployment, income, incidence of poverty and
demographic statistics. Statistical knowledge or

84

background would be helpful in reviewing the
information in this report.

Vallé, Ramon, editor. The Elder: Cross-Cultural
    Study of Minority Elders in San Diego. San
    Diego, CA: Center on Aging, San Diego State
    University. Campanile Press, 1978.
    A series of reports on the ethnic aged in San
Diego. The reports are published individually, but
are uniform in research methodology and presentation.
Each volume includes full bibliographies, usually
annotated. The titles are:
    Cheng, Eva. The Elder Chinese
    Dukepoo, Frank. The Elder American Indian
    Ishikawa, Wesley. The Elder Guamanian
    Ishikawa, Wesley. The Elder Samoan
    Ishizuka, Karen. The Elder Japanese
    Peterson, Roberta. The Elder Pilipino
    Stanford, E. Percil. The Elder Black
    Vallè, Ramon; and Mendoza, Lydia. The Elder
        Latino

ARTICLES

Cantor, Marjorie H. "Effect of Ethnicity on Life
    Styles of the Inner-City Elderly." In M. Powell
    Lawton, Robert J. Newcomer, and Thomas O. Byert,
    editors. Community Planning for the Aging
    Society. Stroudsburg, PA: Dowden, Hutchinson
    and Ross, 1976.
    Based on a survey conducted among New York City
lower-income elderly of black, Hispanic and white
origins. Author assesses family relationships,
income, and housing patterns, and concludes that in
some areas at least ethnicity makes a difference in
the aging process.

Dowd, James J.; and Bengtson, Vern L. "Aging in
    Minority Populations: An Examination of the
    Double Jeopardy Hypothesis." Journal of
    Gerontology 33 (1978): 427-436.
    A useful restatement and critique, using data
from Los Angeles, of a frequently cited theoretical
position: that the ethnic elderly suffer from
"double jeopardy"--being old and the member of a
minority group. Authors found only mixed support
for the hypothesis.

Erlich, Ira F. "The Aged Black in America: The
    Forgotten Person." Journal of Negro Education
    44 (1975): 12-23.

A short discussion of the status of black
elderly with suggestions by the author for improved
social policy and education. Erlich reviews his own
research in St. Louis.

_____. "Toward a Social Profile of the Aged
    Black Population in the United States: An
    Exploratory Study." International Journal of
    Aging and Human Development 4 (1973): 271-276.
    A report of a St. Louis study of the activity
of older blacks. Erlich found the general pattern
to be individual activity rather than group
involvement. He further suggests that the influence
of race on some social statistics may be mitigated
by socio-economic status.

Fandetti, Donald; and Gelfand, Donald. "Care of the
    Aged: Attitudes of White Ethnic Families."
    The Gerontologist 16 (1976): 544-549.
    One of the very few articles on white ethnic
elderly. Based on surveys of elderly Polish and
Italian-American adults and their middle-aged
children. Found that a strong sense of family
obligation was still the norm, although families of
higher socio-economic status were more willing to
resort to non-ethnic care.

The Gerontologist 11: 1 Part II (1971): 26-98.
    A special issue on ethnicity that includes
several theoretical pieces, as well as articles on
Mexican-American, Asian-American, and black elderly;
widows; and inner city elderly.

Jackson, Jacquelyne J. "The Blacklands of
    Gerontology." Aging and Human Development 2
    (1971): 156-171; and

_____. "Social Gerontology and the Negro: A
    Review." The Gerontologist 7 (1967): 168-78.
    Jackson is the most prolific writer on black
aging. The 1967 review of the literature was the
first of its kind, updated by the 1971 piece. Both
are extremely useful and comprehensive as state-of-
the art essays.

Kalish, Richard; and Yuen, Sam. "Americans of East
    Asian Ancestry: Aging and the Aged." The
    Gerontologist 12 (1972): 36-47.
    Kalish is another well-known name in the area
of ethnicity and aging and he has co-authored several
articles on elderly Asian Americans. This one

considers different nationalities within the larger
group, reviews current research and speculates on
the problems of doing ethnic research.

Keith, Jennie, special editor. Anthropological
    Quarterly 52: 1 (1979).
    An issue devoted to anthropological research in
contemporary American residential communities for
the aged. Ethnicity was a factor considered by
nearly all the authors and Keith speculates on its
possibly changing significance in such settings.

Woehrer, Carol. "Cultural Pluralism in American
    Families: The Influence of Ethnicity on Social
    Aspects of Aging." The Family Coordinator 27
    (1978): 329-339.
    A skillful review of the way family
relationships, and attitudes toward older members,
vary according to ethnic group. Although the author
relies heavily on one anthology for her information,
other sources and theoretical perspectives are
integrated into the essay.

FAMILY, FRIENDS, AND NEIGHBORS

The family has in a sense been "rediscovered"
in recent years and recognized as being vitally
important to many old people. Interest in the role
the family plays has been broadened and subsumed
under the general category of support networks which
may include friends and neighbors as well as family.
These support networks may serve as a buffer between
the older individual and the rest of society;
certainly they are an important source of assistance
and emotional solace. There are not many full-length
monographs on the subject, indicating its relatively
recent emergence as a significant topic, but there
is a large body of journal literature and most
social science gerontology books include at least
one chapter on family and friends of the elderly.
There are also a considerable number of books on the
aged and their families which can be classified as
self-help works. In addition to the gerontological
literature, the Journal of Marriage and the Family
has published a number of papers on the family life
of the elderly.

FAMILY, FRIENDS, AND NEIGHBORS:
ANNOTATED REFERENCES

One should begin research by looking at an
excellent review of the literature:

Lillian Troll. "The Family of Later Life: A
      Decade Review." Journal of Marriage and the
      Family. 33 (1971): 263-290.
      Although now a decade old, this review remains
an excellent introduction to the field. It is a
selective review of the sociological and social
psychological literature of the 1960's on the
American family. Most of the review deals with
kinship ties of older people, kinship structure,
and kinship interaction. The achievement of the
1960's is seen here as the recognition of the
importance of extended kin relations and the
continued contact between aging individuals and their
kin, particularly their children. Troll organizes
the review according to variables which most
frequently appear in the studies (e.g. residential
propinquity, marital relations, economic
interdependence, etc.).

BOOKS

Bane, Mary Jo. Here to Stay: American Families
      in the Twentieth Century. New York: Basic
      Books, 1976.
      While the elderly is but one topic discussed
here, Part II, "Commitments in Conflict," provides
an admirably clear and judicious discussion of
complex issues that increasingly affect the family
relations of the elderly in a rapidly aging society:
family privacy, family responsibility, social
values, and the dilemmas of governmental family
policy.

Bott, Elizabeth. Family and Social Network.
      London: Tavistock Publications, 1957.
      Like Bane's work, this is a general piece that
does not focus specifically on the aged. It is
frequently cited, however, by authors who do write
on the elderly and their families--evidence of its
theoretical usefulness. It is based on fieldwork
among English families.

Lopata, Helena Z. Widowhood in an American City.
      Cambridge, MA: Schenkman Publishing, 1973.
      A classic study by one of the best known

writers in the field. Lopata examined the lives of
Chicago widows aged fifty and over from the
perspective of social role and considered the
women's relations with children, kin, friends, and
the larger community. She used a cross-cultural
approach, pointing up differences among various
ethnic groups. Findings are carefully summarized.
There is a useful methodological section on
fieldwork and a good bibliography. The
questionnaires employed in the study are included.

_____. Women as Widows: Support Systems. New
     York: Elsevier, 1979.
     A continuation of Lopata's interest in the
experiences of widows. She again focuses on Chicago
widows basing her conclusions on interviews done in
1970. The theoretical perspective is the role of
support systems in the lives of these women. How
does a widow employ social, community, and personal
resources to establish support systems that will
meet economic, service, social, and emotional needs?
This is a careful, comprehensive study; the
questionnaire is included with a useful
bibliography.

Shanas, Ethel; and Streib, Gordon, editors. Social
     Structure and the Family: Generational
     Relations. Englewood Clifts, NJ: Prentice
     Hall, 1965.
     An interdisciplinary, cross-cultural volume of
essays on the three generational family. There are
theoretical discussions as well as reports of
empirical studies. These papers were intended for
fellow professionals and represent a state-of-the-
art at the time. The book will probably be most
useful to advanced students and researchers.

_____; and Sussman, Marvin B., editors. Family,
     Bureaucracy and the Elderly. Durham, NC:
     Duke University Press, 1977.
     According to the editors, "the major theme of
this volume is the linkage of aged persons with
bureaucratic organizations in complex societies and
the role of family networks in such linkages." The
papers were prepared for a 1973 conference and
range from theoretical and interpretive pieces to
empirical studies.

Townsend, Peter. The Family Life of Old People.
     London: Routledge and Kegan, Paul, 1957.
     Although old, this is a still frequently cited

work. It is a field study of the family
relationships of working class elderly in East
London. Townsend was an early advocate of the
argument that the elderly are not necessarily cut
off from their families in modern society.

Troll, Lillian E; Miller, S. J.; and Atchley, Robert
    C. Families in Later Life. Belmont, CA:
    Wadsworth Publishing Co., 1978.
    A clearly-written brief survey of the subject,
providing an excellent up-to-date source for readers
new to the field. Particularly attractive are the
authors' balanced comments bearing on theory, as
well as on their subject's implications for public
policy, counseling, the academic community, and
for the lay public. There is an extensive list of
references.

ARTICLES

Cantor, Marjorie H. "Neighbors and Friends: An
    Overlooked Resource in the Informal Support
    System." Research on Aging. I (1979): 434-
    463.
    Cantor has led a major research project on the
elderly in New York City and has written a number
of articles based on the results of that research.
Her special focus is frequently the support, or
helping, networks of the aged. This article
discusses the role of non-kin, and considers those
situations when the elderly person turns to friends
or neighbors rather than kin. Several theoretical
models are presented along with the author's own
proposal for a new model.

Hess, Beth B.; and Waring, Joan M. "Changing
    Patterns of Aging and Family Bonds in Later
    Life." The Family Coordinator, 27 (1978):
    303-314.
    A critical review of demographic trends and the
research literature pointing to a transition from
relations between elderly parents and their children
based on obligation to relations based upon
voluntary interaction, assumed and maintained by
both aged parents and their adult children. See for
analysis of factors that both enhance and detract
from intergenerational relations; also for the
relationship between intergenerational relations and
life satisfaction of the aged.

90

Rosenmayer, Leopold. "Family Relations of the
    Elderly," Journal of Marriage and the Family.
    30 (1968): 672-680.
    A frequently cited article which predates the
current interest in support systems. The author
reviewed findings from a number of European
countries and concluded, contrary to widely held
belief, that kinship ties remain important in modern
society manifested as "intimacy at a distance." He
suggested theoretical links between social
gerontology and the sociology of the family.

Tobin, Sheldon S. "The Mystique of Deinstitutuionali-
    zation." Society, 15 (1978): 73-75.
    A brief but stimulating questioning of the
workability of deinstitutionalizing elderly people,
discussed in the context of the need for innovative
alternatives to institutional care. See in relation
to Sussman (1976) and Troll, et al. (1978), 134-136.

Ward, Russell A. "Limitations of the Family As a
    Supportive Institution in the Lives of the
    Aged." Family Coordinator, 27 (1978): 365-
    373.
    A lucid discussion of the roles the extended
family can and cannot play in the lives of aged
members, both now and in the future. The author's
main thesis is that the family is especially
effective in acute emergency situations, but ill-
suited to providing long-term aid. Family policy
should account for the variety of family life, and
should support effective family functioning where
it exists, and support alternatives where it is
absent.

Woehrer, Carol. "Cultural Pluralism in American
    Families: The Influence of Ethnicity on
    Social Aspects of Aging." The Family
    Coordinator 27 (1978): 329-339.
    (see annotation, p. 86).

POLITICS AND POLICY

    The part old people play in political life has
two dimensions: the policies created by government
that affect the lives of the elderly, and the
political involvement of old people themselves.
Both dimensions have become increasingly important
in recent years as the numbers of old people in the
population have grown. There are only a few
monographs on aging and politics, a reflection

perhaps of the relatively recent interest in the
subject. There is, however, a large body of
periodical literature, much of which has appeared
in political science publications. Political
scientists have made important contributions to
methodological development in gerontology,
particularly in the area of cohort analysis. In
addition to the gerontological and political science
journals, some of the standard political science
texts and monographs include sections on aging.

POLITICS AND POLICY: ANNOTATED REFERENCES

BOOKS

Calhoun, Richard B. In Search of the New Old:
    Redefining Old Age in America, 1945-1970. New
    York: Elsevier North-Holland, 1978.
    An interesting attempt to explain changes in
society's perception of the aged as the result of
deliberate efforts by "social engineers" (gerontologists, business leaders, educators, advertisers,
social workers, and labor leaders). An account of
social reform in a pluralist society with policy
presumably affected by these changes. While one
may challenge some of the conclusions, the book is
useful for its presentation of a vast body of
information relative to theoretical and practical
changes in perceptions of the elderly.

Donahue, Wilma; and Tibbits, Clark, editors.
    Politics of Age. Ann Arbor: University of
    Michigan Press, 1962.
    An early collection of papers presented at a
1961 conference on the "Politics of Age." There are
a number of papers on political behavior and
participation of the elderly; considerably less
attention to role of government and the development
of old age policy.

Eisele, Frederick R., editor. "Political
    Consequences of Aging." The Annals of the
    American Academy of Political and Social
    Science 415 (1974).
    A well-known and significant issue featuring
prominent writers in the field who examined public
policy, political behavior and prospects for the
future. There are articles on income maintenance,
service delivery, pensions, nursing homes, area
agencies on aging, old age associations, black
elderly, political attitudes of the elderly, and

92

age differences within the elderly population.

Holtzman, Abraham. The Townsend Movement: A
    Political Study. New York: Basic Books, 1963.
    This is a history of one of the earliest
organized expressions of "old age politics" in the
United States. The Townsend movement for old age
economic security swelled during the Great
Depression and then dwindled to a relatively few
adherents in later years. Holtzman analyzes the
structure and politics of the movement, suggests
reasons for its decline and reflects on present-
day (1960's) old-age politics.

Kasschau, Patricia L. Aging and Social Policy:
    Leadership Planning. New York: Praeger, 1978.
    An investigation of the ways decision makers
shape and implement social policy for the aged. The
author conducted wide ranging interviews with
legislators, administrators, social workers,
corporate and union leaders and representatives of
the elderly. The study covered a five year period,
and results indicated discrepancies between
reported and perceived needs.

McKinney, John C.; and de Vyver, Frank, editors.
    Aging and Social Policy. New York: Appleton-
    Century-Crofts, 1966.
    A collection of papers written for a symposium
at Duke University in 1965 by participants in the
Program in Socio-Economic Studies of Aging. The
papers present the relationship of the elderly to
social, political and economic systems, and
highlight certain topics of special consequence to
the development of public policy: retirement,
employment and income, public programming, social
services, housing, health care, institutionalization,
and death. These are thought pieces which, although
a bit dated, present vital issues and suggest
possible directions for a national policy toward the
aged.

Pinner, Frank A.; Jacobs, Paul; and Selznick, Philip.
    Old Age and Political Behavior: A Case Study.
    Berkeley: University of California Press,
    1959.
    A study of the pension movement in California
led by George H. McLain. Although it had its roots
in the Depression, the movement developed in the
1940's and was ongoing at the time of field work and
survey research conducted by the authors. The book

is decidedly dated in rhetoric and methodology, but provides some interesting insight to this dimension of politics and aging.

Pratt, Henry J. The Gray Lobby. Chicago: The
    University of Chicago Press, 1976.
    A history of old age policy formulation since the late 1920's. The book considers trends, analyzes the elderly as a power group, and considers possible constraints to political action. This is a well-documented account of a major movement within American society.

Wolfgang, Marvin E., editor. "Planning for the
    Elderly." The Annals of the American Academy
    of Political and Social Science. 438 (1978).
    A collection of essays that consider the facts of an aging society and the obligations of social policy to the old. The issue includes articles on the family, alternatives to institutional care, mandatory retirement, assessment of functional status, leisure activities, police services, and problems for future policy makers.

ARTICLES

Abramson, P. R. "Generational Change in American
    Electoral Behavior." American Political
    Science Review 68 (1974): 93-105.
    Abramson has been principally concerned with the changes in American political life as one voting generation gives way to another. He argues that younger generations are increasingly divided along partisan issue lines rather than social class.

Binstock, Robert H. "Interest-Group Liberalism and
    the Politics of Aging." The Gerontologist 12
    (1972): 265-280.
    A frequently cited article by a political scientist well-known in gerontology. The author analyzes the role in Washington of representatives of various senior citizens groups and organizations, and the relationship that has developed between those representatives and various federal agencies. He suggests that by concentrating on such well-established interest groups, federal policies may be failing to meet the needs of many elderly individuals.

94

Cutler, Neal E. "Demographic, Social Psychological
and Political Factors in the Politics of Aging,
A Foundation for Research in 'Political
Gerontology.'" American Political Review 71
(1977): 1011-1026.
This thought piece represents a call to
political scientists to seriously consider political
gerontology and its relationship to other
disciplines.

Pratt, Henry J. "Politics of Aging: Political
Science and the Study of Gerontology."
Research on Aging I (1979): 155-186.
An extremely helpful "state of the art" review
of political gerontology from the perspective of
political science. Pratt covers the period 1950 to
the present and highlights both substantive and
methodological developments. There are discussions
of important works in the field.

SEXUALITY AND AGING

This is a subject that has attracted considerable interest in recent years. It is a topic that
has been shrouded in myth and taboo, and much of the
literature is devoted to dispelling stereotypes.
The body of writings is relatively small, but there
is a good selection of responsible, scholarly
research, most of which reflects medical,
psychological and sociological perspectives.

SEXUALITY AND AGING: ANNOTATED REFERENCES

BOOKS

Burnside, Irene Mortenson, editor. Sexuality and
Aging. Los Angeles: Andrus Gerontology Center,
University of Southern California, 1975.
A short, interdisciplinary volume. Articles
cover such matters as the implications of sexuality
for nursing home residents, physical changes, and
psycho-social considerations. The book is intended
for a general audience, particularly service
providers to the aged. There is an excellent
bibliography that includes a short list of films.

Butler, Robert; and Lewis, Myrna. Sex After Sixty:
A Guide for Men and Women in Their Later Years.
New York: Harper and Row, 1976.
A comprehensive and practical description of

the role of human sexual expression for persons in
the later stages of life. Good discussion of the
physiological, psychological, and social changes to
be expected, problems and dysfunctions which might
occur, and suggestions for action which might lead
to enhancement and enrichment of sexual expression.

Felstein, Ivor. Sex and the Longer Life. London:
    Allen Lane Penguin Press, 1970.
    Felstein is an English geriatric physician who
has written a short, engaging volume designed to
refute myths and stereotypes about sexuality in
later life. He uses clinical examples throughout
as he discusses physical changes and reviews current
medical and psychological knowledge. He considers
popular expectations and beliefs and their impact
on the lives of older people.

Peterson, James A.; and Payne, Barbara. Love in the
    Later Years: The Emotional, Sexual and Social
    Potential of the Elderly. New York:
    Association Press, 1975.
    Using case studies, this book examines love,
sex and marriage in later life. It touches on other
matters, such as economics, which may affect a
relationship. The book takes an optimistic stance
and is designed for a general audience including
beginning researchers, service providers and the
aged.

                    ARTICLES

    There are a number of general works concerning
human sexuality that have good chapters on aging:

Berman, Ellen M.; and Lief, Harold I. "Sex and the
    Aging Process." In Sex and the Life Cycle,
    edited by Wilbur W. Oaks, Gerald A.
    Melchiode, and Ilda Ficher. New York: Grune
    and Stratton, 1976: 125-134.
    Examines human sexual expression throughout a
person's life cycle yielding a sound perspective on
the role that sexuality plays in growth and
development. Affirms the validity of sexual
expression in the aging process. The chapter on
aging is good, but the most value will be derived
from reading the entire book, thus placing
sexuality in the life span perspective.

Masters, William; and Johnson, Virginia. "The
    Aging Female," and "The Aging Male." In Human

Sexual Response, by William Masters and
Virginia Johnson. Boston: Little, Brown,
1966: 223-272; and

_____. "Sexual Inadequacy in the Aging Male,"
and "Sexual Inadequacy in the Aging Female."
In Human Sexual Inadequacy, by William Masters
and Virginia Johnson. Boston: Little, Brown,
1970: 316-350.

The two volumes by Masters and Johnson give an
excellent data resource regarding sexuality and
aging, especially with respect to the physiological
expectations. The chapters on potential problems
are useful, both in terms of the typical difficulties
and changes encountered and the resources available
for problem resolution. Goes a long way in negating
some of the commonly held myths.

Wasow, Mona; and Loeb, Martin B. "The Aged." In
The Sexually Oppressed, edited by Harvey L.
Gochros and Jean S. Gochros. New York:
Association Press, 1977: 54-68.
A specially hopeful statement about sexuality
and aging, yet clear in terms of the many struggles
encountered due to social attitudes. Good
discussion of some of the institutional issues in
aging, especially in terms of nursing home expenses.
Contains good bibliography and numerous other
chapters of related interest, such as: "The
Handicapped, Ill, and Dying."

5
Environments and the Elderly

The study of the individual's relationship to the environment has attracted the interest of many disciplines: geography, psychology, urban planning and design, architecture, and, of course, gerontology. Physical changes associated with growing old frequently affect the ability of older people to successfully negotiate their environment. There is a large body of literature--much of it outside the usual gerontological sources--that examines a wide variety of environmental issues: perception and mobility, housing, transportation, migration, and institutionalization. Perhaps because it has been more feasible to study old people residing in congregate settings such as retirement villages and nursing homes, much of the literature reports on this type of environment. However, there has been an increasing interest in the lives of old people who remain in the community at large, a vast majority of the elderly population. This interest extends to the planning of manageable environments that will enable older people to continue functioning effectively in the community setting. Research ranges from studies of an individual in a room or building, to large scale examinations of a total environment (the neighborhood or city) in which a person carries out a wide range of activities. A number of creative methodologies have been developed that enable researchers to assess use of resources and movement within a particular environment.

ENVIRONMENT AND THE ELDERLY: ANNOTATED REFERENCES

The following works represent a general and theoretical approach to the subject.

BOOKS

Byerts, Thomas O.; Howell, Sandra C.; and
    Pastalan, Leon A. Environmental Context of
    Aging: Life-Styles, Environmental Quality,
    and Living Arrangements. New York: Garland
    STPM Press, 1979.
This recent collection of essays has a social
science (rather than a design or planning)
perspective. It is an excellent introduction to the
subject which presents many of the key issues in
environmental research, theory and policy. There
are essays on city and rural aged, support systems,
environmental design, sensory changes, transportation
and driving, and specialized environments for the
aged.

_____. Environmental Research and Aging.
    Washington, DC: Gerontological Society, 1974.
A companion to the Windley et al. reference
below. This volume describes the main approaches
to empirical research associated with environments
and the elderly. (Both texts are coming out in
revised, hardcover editions.)

Golant, Stephen M. The Residential Location and
    Spatial Behavior of the Elderly: A Canadian
    Example. University of Chicago: Department of
    Geography Research Paper #143, Chicago, 1972.
A good case study that gives special attention
to two types of environmental behavior--residential
migration and daily trip activity. The author
examined movement as well as the decision making
processes that initiated the movement. The study
and results are described in detail.

Gubrium, Jaber F. The Myth of the Golden Years: A
    Socio-Environmental Theory of Aging.
    Springfield, IL: Charles C. Thomas, 1973.
Gubrium has elaborated a "socio-environmental
theory of aging" which was prompted by what he
perceived to be the inadequacies of the activity and
disengagement theories. His theory is "ego
centered"; that is, it describes the relationship
between the individual and his/her environment.
Although he acknowledges the individual's ability
to cope and to change environments when necessary,
Gubrium takes a point of view common to many in
gerontology: the old person is acted upon by the
environment.

_____, editor. Late Life: Communities and
Environmental Policy. Springfield, IL: Charles
C. Thomas, 1974.
This is a collection of original essays on
various aspects of the environment and the elderly.
Discussions focus on four dimensions of old-age
environments: the physical environment, formal
communities, cross-cultural communities, and
environmental policy.

Kira, Alexander. The Bathroom. New York: Viking,
1976.
Presents a more molecular approach. Kira
conducted a series of studies devoted to the
evaluation of bathrooms from a behavioral
perspective. This same approach could be used to
find out how best to design kitchens, entrances,
appliances, and motor vehicles for the older
population.

Lawton, M. Powell; Newcomer, Robert J.; and Byerts,
Thomas O., editors. Community Planning for an
Aging Society. Stroudsburg, PA: Dowden,
Hutchinson and Ross, 1976.
This volume is a product of the same group that
wrote Environmental Context of Aging, and is of the
same high quality. It is a collection of original
essays with an emphasis on the application of
environmental psychology to planning and design
needs for the elderly. There are discussions of the
community environment, demography, ethnicity,
transportation, housing, service delivery, and
environmental planning.

Michelson, William H. Man and His Urban Environment:
A Sociological Approach. Reading, MA: Addison-
Wesley Publishing, 1970.
A general theoretical work that does not focus
specifically on the aged, but provides a stimulating
discussion of human ecology. Many of Michelson's
observations apply to the urban elderly. There is
a good bibliography.

Pastalan, Leon A.; and Carson, Daniel H., editors.
Spatial Behavior of Older People. Ann Arbor,
MI: University of Michigan-Wayne State
University Institute of Gerontology, 1970.
This is a collection of twelve papers from a
1968 conference. The discussions present both
theoretical and experimental results, and cover such
topics as territoriality, home range, adaptation to

change, privacy, crowding, and environmental design.
The emphasis is largely on elderly in congregate
settings rather than in the community. Included is
a widely cited study by Robert Sommer on seating
arrangement and conversation in a day room. There
are useful, although now somewhat dated
bibliographies at the end of each essay.

Rowles, Graham D. Prisoners of Space? Exploring
    the Geographical Experience of Older People.
    Boulder, CO: Westview Press, 1978.
    This is the report of a two year study
described as "an in-depth exploration of the
geographical experience, defined as 'involvement
within the spaces and places of their lives,'" of
five elderly persons who have lived for many years
in a workingclass inner city neighborhood. The
author uses vignettes to document the changing
relationship of an older person with the environment.

Windley, Paul G.; Byerts, Thomas O.; and Ernst, F.
    Gene, editors. Theory Development in
    Environment and Aging. Washington, DC:
    Gerontological Society, 1975.
    A good review of the current state of theory
development in this area.

Wiseman, Robert F. Spatial Aspects of Aging.
    Washington, DC: Association for American
    Geographers, 1978.
    This is a short, readable monograph that
synthesizes relevant literature in the field and
presents it from a geographical perspective. There
are discussions of special "geographical" questions:
elderly population growth and distribution; migration
patterns; environmental issues; service delivery;
transportation systems. There is a long,
comprehensive bibliography.

ARTICLES

Byerts, Thomas O., Guest editor. Journal of
    Architectural Education 31: 1(1977).
    The entire issue is devoted to discussions of
environmental planning and design for the aged.
The articles will probably be most useful to the
advanced student and professional.

Longino, Charles F., Jr.; and Jackson, David J.,
    editors. "Aged Migration in the United States."
    Special Issue: Research on Aging. II: 2(1980).

An issue devoted to a major topic of research in environmental studies--migration. Articles include theoretical, methodological and empirical discussions.

Norris-Baker, C.; and Willems, E. P. "Environmental Negotiability As A Direct Measurement of Behavior-Environment Relationships." In A. D. Seidel and S. Danford, editors. Environmental Design: Research, Theory, and Application. Washington, DC: Environmental Design Research Association, 1979.
Shows how the concept of environmental negotiability can be of value in analyzing everyday environments. This work was conducted with persons who have suffered spinal cord injuries. It could just as easily have dealt with the elderly. The environmental negotiability survey is described. Explanation is given as to how the survey can provide accurate data regarding behavior-environment relationships.

Schooler, Kermit K. "Environmental Change and the Elderly." In Irwin Altman and Joachim F. Wohlwill, editors. Human Behavior and Environment: Advances in Theory and Research. Vol. I. New York: Plenum, 1976, pp. 265-298.
Good review of the impact of environmental change on older persons. Includes voluntary and involuntary relocation (e.g. the move from private residence to a nursing home) and subsequent effects on satisfaction, health, and mortality.

Snyder, Lorraine Hiatt. "The Environmental Challenge and the Aging Individual." Council of Planning Librarians Bibliography #254. Monticello, IL: Council of Planning Librarians, 1972.
A good review essay of the literature followed by an annotated bibliography.

COMMUNITY AND CONGREGATE SETTINGS

BOOKS

Brody, Elaine. Long-Term Care of Older People: A Practical Guide. New York: Human Sciences Press, 1977.
Although intended for service providers, this volume provides a good background for the general reader. There are discussions of the history of nursing homes and the assumptions underlying

long-term care of the aged. There are a number of suggestions for what "ought to be" as contrasted with the present or past situation.

Carp, Frances. A Future for the Aged: The Residents of Victoria Plaza. Austin, TX: University of Texas Press, 1966.
    A classic study of a successful public housing project for the aged in San Antonio, Texas. Carp was interested in the psychological well being of the residents, their quality of life, and the nature of their social interaction.

Dunlop, Burton David. The Growth of Nursing Home Care. Lexington, MA: Lexington Books, 1979.
    A report of case studies of nursing homes in ten states. The author analyzes policies, patterns of growth, quality of care, and public financial support and regulation. The principal aim is to account for the greatly increased use of nursing homes in this country. The methodology is explained and the results presented in extensive appendices.

Gubrium, Jaber. Living and Dying at Murray Manor. New York: St. Martin's Press, 1975.
    A sociological description of life in a home for the aged. The author details the routine of the residents, clinical and maintenance staff, and administration. A clearly written case study, useful for college students at all levels.

Hochschild, Arlie Russell. The Unexpected Community: Portrait of An Old Age Subculture. Berkeley: University of California Press, 1973.
    A report of a three year study begun in 1966 of a low-income apartment building in the San Francisco area. The forty-three elderly residents formed a community, and the author provides a full description of the social relationships, mutual aid, customs and traditions, and living arrangements of the group. This is a readable, engaging account accompanied by a good bibliography.

Jacobs, Jerry. Fun City--An Ethnographic Study of a Retirement Community. New York: Holt, Rinehart and Winston, 1974.
    A short case study, employing the methods and perspective of cultural anthropology, of a planned community inhabited by white, middle class retirees. There is a considerable emphasis in the community on activity. The author concluded that Fun City was

characterized by both social and geographic
isolation. He relates his findings to various
gerontological theories.

Manard, Barbara Bolling; Woehle, Ralph E.; Heilman,
James M. Better Homes for the Old. Lexington,
MA: Lexington Books, 1977.
An analysis of old-age institutions in the
United States in light of the changes that have
occurred with the shift from private to largely
public support. The report is based on in-depth
studies in three states: Massachusetts, Virginia,
and Utah. The authors suggest that while old-age
institutions have improved dramatically, they tend
to be organized according to a medical model that
views old people as patients rather than residents.
The report considers the implications of this
attitude and other policy-related issues.

Niebanck, Paul L. The Elderly in Older Urban Areas:
Problems of Adaptation and the Effects of
Relocation. Philadelphia: Institute for
Environmental Studies, University of
Pennsylvania, 1965.
A dated, but still cited national study of the
effect of forcible relocation due to urban renewal
and redevelopment on elderly residents. The author
provides a demographic profile of the elderly, and
discusses housing needs, psychological considerations,
and some relocation programs.

Ross, Jennie-Keith. Old People, New Lives:
Community Creation in a Retirement Residence.
Chicago: University of Chicago Press, 1977.
An anthropological study of life in a French
retirement home in the early 1970's. The author
employed participant-observation techniques to study
the nature of the community that formed in a
homogeneous residence setting. A sensitive,
readable study.

Smith, Bert Kruger. The Pursuit of Dignity: New
Living Alternatives for the Elderly. Boston:
Beacon Press, 1977.
A volume intended for lay audiences that
provides a discussion of various alternatives for
maintaining independence on the part of the elderly.
The author provides an overview of services and
living arrangements such as day care, home health,
co-operative housing, and nutrition centers.

104

Stephens, Joyce. <u>Loners, Losers and Lovers: Elderly
Tenants in a Slum Hotel</u>. Seattle: University
of Washington Press, 1976.
A participant observation study of the elderly
residents of a single room occupancy (SRO) slum hotel
in a midwestern city. This is a report of old
people living in extremely difficult circumstances
who nevertheless demonstrated remarkable abilities
to cope. There is a good methodology chapter.

Tobin, Sheldon S.; and Lieberman, Morton A. <u>Last
Home for the Aged: Critical Implications of
Institutionalization</u>. San Francisco: Jossey-
Bass, 1976.
A report of the results of intensive interviews
with eighty-five elderly people before and after
admission to a sectarian home for the aged. The
author was particularly concerned with testing
commonly held assumptions and stereotypes about the
effects of institutionalization. The author
discusses the implications of his results for
practice. The measures developed and used in the
study are included in the Appendix; there is a useful
bibliography.

Townsend, Clair. <u>Old Age: The Last Segregation</u>.
New York: Bantam Books, 1971.
The Ralph Nader Study Group Report on Nursing
Homes. Young researchers examined the conditions
of nursing homes in early 1970. There is an
emphasis on the abuses and negative aspects of these
institutions and on aging in general. The report
includes recommendations and suggestions for change.

ARTICLES

Brody, Elaine M. "Congregate Care Facilities and
Mental Health of the Elderly." <u>Aging and Human
Development</u> I (1970): 279-321.
A full discussion of the issues related to
institutionalized care. The author reviews present
conditions in general and uses one facility in
Philadelphia as an example of current practice. An
extensive bibliography is included. See also a
symposium on the Community Housing project and
related programs, <u>The Gerontologist</u> 18 (1978): 121-
158.

Byerts, Thomas O., special editor and organizer.
"The City: A Viable Environment for the
Elderly?" <u>The Gerontologist</u> 15 (1975): 13-46.

A series of articles by prominent researchers
in the field who participated in a four year (HEW
sponsored) study project in the early 1970's.
Discussions focus on the urban elderly in various
regions of the country. Topics include: support
systems, policy and planning, and life-style.

Bultena, Gordon L. and Wood, Vivian. "The American
     Retirement Community: Bane or Blessing?"
     Journal of Gerontology 24 (1969): 209-217.
     A frequently cited study of age integration
versus age segregation. The authors analyzed levels
of morale among the aged male residents of both
types of retirement settings in Arizona.

Gottesman, Leonard E., symposium editor and organizer.
     "Symposium--Long Term Care: Research, Policy,
     and Practice." The Gerontologist 14 (1974):
     494-524.
     A series of articles that address such issues
as relocation of nursing home patients,
accountability of institutions, and ways of
improving long term care.

Hartman, C.; Horovitz, J.; and Herman, R. "Designing
     with the Elderly." The Gerontologist 16 (1976):
     303-311.
     Describes an interesting survey of housing
needs for a population of older people in San
Francisco. The results of such surveys can be
used to develop design guidelines for architects and
planners who design for older persons.

Gruber, Herman W. "History of Nursing Homes--A
     Review." In The Extended Care Facility: A
     Handbook for the Medical Staff. Chicago:
     American Medical Association, 1967: 115-126.
     A good survey and history of the nursing home
movement that identifies changes and developments in
recent years.

Reader, George G. "Types of Geriatric Institutions."
     The Gerontologist 13 (1973): 290-294.
     A survey of the types of old age institutions
available in the United States with some cross-
cultural comparison.

ENVIRONMENTS AND THE ELDERLY
OTHER REFERENCES (GENERAL)

BOOKS

Warnes, A. M., Editor. Geographical Aspects of
Ageing. London: John Wiley and Sons, 1980.

ARTICLES

The following articles would provide a useful
introduction to the subject, and are representative
of some of the leading writers in the field.

Blenkner, Margaret. "Environmental Change and the
    Aging Individual." The Gerontologist 7:2
    (1967): 101-105.

Carp, Frances M. "The Impact of Environment on Old
    People." The Gerontologist   7:2   (1967):
    106-108.

Golant, Stephen M. "Residential Concentrations of
    the Future Elderly." The Gerontologist 15:1
    (1975): 16-23.

Lawton, M. Powell; and Simon, Bonnie. "The Ecology
    of Social Relationships in Housing for the
    Elderly." The Gerontologist 8 (1968): 108-115.

Peet, Richard; and Rowles, Graham. "Geographical
    Aspects of Aging." The Geographical Review.
    4074 (1978).

THE ELDERLY IN COMMUNITY AND CONGREGATE
SETTINGS

BOOKS

Atchley, Robert; and Byerts, Thomas O., editors.
    Rural Environments and Aging. Washington, DC:
    Gerontological Society, 1975.

Belfer, O.; and Nierstraz, F. N. S. Housing the
    Aged in Western Countries. Amsterdam:
    Elsevier, 1967.

Cantilli, Edmund J.; and Shmelzer, June L., editors.
    Transportation and Aging: Selected Issues.

Based on Proceedings of the Interdisciplinary
Workshop on Transportation and Aging,
Washington, DC: U. S. Government Printing
Office, 1970.

Langford, M. Community Aspects of Housing for the
Aged. Ithaca, NY: Cornell University Center
for Housing and Environmental Studies, 1962.

Lawton, M. Powell. Planning and Managing Housing
for the Elderly. New York: Wiley-Interscience,
1975.

U.S. Department of Health, Education and Welfare.
Transportation for the Elderly: The State of
the Art. Washington, DC: Department of HEW,
Office of Human Development, Administration on
Aging DHEW Publication No. (OHD) 75-20081,
1975.

U.S. Senate Report. Trends in Long Term Care.
Hearings before the Subcommittee on Long Term
Care of the Special Committee on Aging. U.S.
Senate, 91st Congress. Washington, DC: U.S.
Government Printing Office, 1971.

ARTICLES

Blenkner, Margaret. "The Place of the Nursing Home
Among Community Resources." Journal of
Geriatric Psychiatry I (1967): 135-144.

Hiltner, John; and Smith, Bruce N. "Location
Patterns of the Urban Elderly: Are They
Segregated?" Great Plains-Rocky Mountain
Geographical Journal 3 (1974): 43-48.

Koncelik, Joseph A. "Considerate Design and the
Aging: Review Article and Annotated
Bibliography." Exchange Bibliography #253.
Monticello, IL: Council of Planning
Librarians, 1972.

Lawton, M. Powell; and Cohen, Jacob. "Environment
and the Well Being of Inner City Residents."
Environment and Behavior 6 (1974): 195-211.

Markovitz, Joanie K. "Transportation Needs of the
Elderly." Traffic Quarterly 25 (1971): 237-
253.

Author Index

Title Index

In this section of the index, all book titles appear in capital letters.

116

AGING AND BEHAVIOR, 60
AGING AND COMMUNICATION: A SELECTED BIBLIOGRAPHIC
  RESEARCH GUIDE, 15
AGING AND INCOME, 76
"Aging and IQ: The Myth of the Twilight Years," 64
AGING AND LEISURE: A RESEARCH PERSPECTIVE INTO THE
  MEANINGFUL USE OF TIME, 49
AGING AND MENTAL DISORDER IN SAN FRANCISCO, 63
AGING AND MENTAL HEALTH: POSITIVE PSYCHOSOCIAL
  APPROACHES,61
AGING AND MODERNIZATION,81
AGING AND NUTRITION, 20
AGING AND SOCIAL POLICY, 49, 92
AGING AND SOCIAL POLICY: LEADERSHIP PLANNING, 92
AGING AND SOCIETY, Vol. I-III, 49
AGING AND THE ECONOMY, 76
AGING AND THE ELDERLY: HUMANISTIC PERSPECTIVES IN
  GERONTOLOGY, 46
AGING AND WORK, 26
"Aging and World-Wide Population Change," 73
"Aging as Exchange: A Preface to Theory," 52
AGING AWARENESS: AN ANNOTATED BIBLIOGRAPHY, 14
AGING BIBLIOGRAPHY, 14
AGING, DEATH AND THE COMPLETION OF BEING, 72
"The Aging Female," 95
AGING FROM BIRTH TO DEATH: INTERDISCIPLINARY
  PERSPECTIVES, 49
AGING IN AMERICA: READINGS IN SOCIAL GERONTOLOGY,
  44
AGING IN CONTEMPORARY SOCIETY, 46
AGING IN MASS SOCIETY: MYTHS AND REALITIES, 43
"Aging in Minority Populations: An Examination of
  the Double Jeopardy Hypothesis," 84
AGING IN TODAY"S SOCIETY, 50
AGING IN WESTERN SOCIETIES, 40
AGING: ITS CHALLENGE TO THE INDIVIDUAL AND TO
  SOCIETY, 39
"The Aging Male," 95
AGING: SCIENTIFIC PERSPECTIVES AND SOCIAL ISSUES,
  48
AGING: SOME SOCIAL AND BIOLOGICAL ASPECTS, 57
THE AGING WORKER AND THE UNION: EMPLOYMENT AND
  RETIREMENT OF MIDDLE AGED AND OLDER WORKERS, 77
ALMOST 65: BASELINE DATA FROM THE RETIREMENT
  HISTORY STUDY, 74
American Association for Geriatric Psychiatry, 30
American Association of Homes for the Aging, 30
American Association of Retired Persons, 30
AMERICAN BEHAVIORAL SCIENTIST - SPECIAL ISSUE, 48
American Geriatrics Society, 31
AMERICAN GERIATRICS SOCIETY - JOURNAL, 27

124

126